STORYTELLING FOR
TURNING FAMILY LINEAGE

by

Doug Tattershall

Genealogical Publishing Company
Baltimore, Maryland

Dedicated to all those members of my family—known and unknown, past and present, loveable and unlovable—who kept, discovered, and passed on our family story.

Copyright © 2024
Doug Tattershall
All Rights Reserved

Published by
Genealogical Publishing Company
Baltimore, Maryland

ISBN 9780806321417

Contents

Why Family Story? ... 1

How to Tell a Good Story ... 5

The Stuff ... 19

Puzzle Pieces ... 33

The Value of Things ... 43

Format ... 51

True and Good ... 63

Before You Write ... 73

Conclusion ... 79

Family Story Worksheet ... 81

Index ... 83

Illustrations

Figure 1. Barbary and Michael Isgrigg, page 3.

Figure 2. The Rev. Benjamin Stevens, page 9.

Figure 3. Jail Escape, page 25.

Figure 4. Belle Brezing in Her Parlor, page 34.

Figure 5. Waterford, Virginia, 1937, page 37.

Figure 6. Waterford, Virginia, today, page 38.

Figure 7. Thomas and Nancy Tattershall, page 44.

Figure 8. *View of Bold Face Creek*, page 45.

Figure 9. Judith Batchelor, page 52.

Figure 10. Keith Gregson, page 54.

Figure 11. Jackie Taylor and Charlotte Campanella, page 57.

Figure 12. Danielle Romero, page 59.

Figure 13. *The Fatal Leap*, page 67.

Why Family Story?

Barbara Lohr was born about 1754, probably in Baltimore County, Maryland, and died on 12 November 1836 in Green Township, Hamilton County, Ohio. She married Michael Isgrigg about 1774 in Baltimore County, Maryland.[1]

Birth, marriage, death. That's it. You're done. You've filled out all the blanks on the chart, and you're ready to move on to the next generation. Your family tree is making good progress.
But surely there's more to it than that.
Does it matter that Barbara and her three oldest children lived with her father while her husband and two brothers fought in the American Revolution, and that her oldest son, while only five, helped capture a loyalist who burned down her father's barn? Does it matter that she and her family traveled to Kentucky on a flatboat captained by William Henry Harrison, later president of the United States? Does it matter that her son drew a picture of her, with a clumsy hand, but a portrait nonetheless?[2]
Of course, it matters.
Genealogy starts with names and dates and places fixed on a chart, but we want to know more than just names and dates and places. We want to know who we really come from. We want to understand what we hold in common with them and what struggles they overcame (or didn't) in order to make our own lives possible. We want to know what burdens they placed on us, what burdens they saved us from, and what burdens we ourselves have happily spared future generations through our own efforts. We want to feel connected to something less fleeting that moves us beyond the present—something timeless.
Creating a family tree is a big undertaking. Filling out all the proper names, dates, and places easily becomes an end in itself. But to really know your ancestors, you'll have to discover something more.
A family tree only hints at it. The dates and places provide clues. However, no family lives in isolation. They're

part of the events and impulses that surround them, sometimes steering those events but more often tossed around by them. And the surnames themselves have meanings often taking us into a family's prehistory. There's a reason a progenitor was named *Smith* even though he wasn't a smith. There's a reason an ancestor was named for a village on a continent he'd never even been to.

The family tree gives us names, but we want to know people. The tree is only a skeleton. We want to put meat on the bone. We want to look our ancestors in the eye, hear what they have to say, and see what kind of impression they make on us.

Sometimes the meat is right there among all those records we pored over in pursuit of our litany of birth, marriage, and death. Sometimes it's waiting to be discovered somewhere else we never thought to look, or never needed to look because it offered nothing toward filling those blanks on the chart.

With genealogy, a life flashes before your eyes, but it isn't your own life. It's someone else's. All those days when someone wasn't born, didn't get married, or didn't die–the vast majority of days in an ancestor's life–pass by unknown. And just as unknown are the people themselves, their character, their personalities, their passions.

A family tree is a particular thing, singular even. Although you find yourself working with others on intertwining lineages, no one is pursuing precisely the same tree. Even interested siblings begin to go in their own directions once they marry.

In other words, part of the drive of genealogy is the fact that if you don't pursue your own family tree, no one else will. The same is true of putting meat on the bone. If you don't find out who your ancestors really were, no one else will. And if you don't tell what you found, no one else will do that either. It's up to you.

That's why it's so important to turn those pedigree charts and family group sheets into a narrative. You're researching your family tree, but you really want to know, and tell, something more. You want to move from the discipline of genealogy to the disciplines of history and biography. This requires a shift–a shift in how you research, a shift in how you think about what you've learned, and a shift in how you present your findings.

The tree gives us names, but we want to know people, and by knowing them we want to know ourselves better. We work hard to discover our family tree. But what we really want to know is our family story.

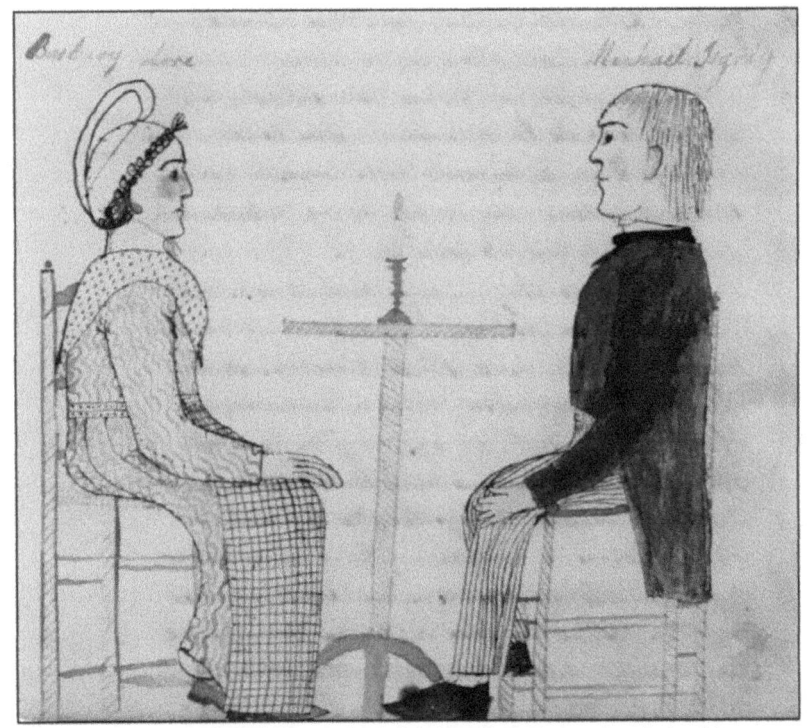

Figure 1. Portrait of Barbary and Michael Isgrigg, drawn by their oldest son, Daniel Isgrigg, in his quirky and revealing handwritten memoir. Courtesy of the Indiana University Lilly Library.

---

[1] *Autobiography of Daniel Isgrig*, unpublished manuscript, 1838, Indiana University Lilly Library, 2. "A Patriarch," *Philadelphia Inquirer*, 13 July 1824. Autobiography gives death date and place; newspaper article gives age.
[2] *Ibid.*

Chapter One
How to Tell a Good Story

A good story engages readers. It keeps them pushing to the story's end. And it leaves them with a lingering experience of the story long after they've finished it. It doesn't matter whether you're reading fiction or nonfiction. The historian and the biographer rely on these ingredients to tell a good story as much as the novelist.

"Solid research and superior style are essential, but even more crucial is narrative form: In most cases non-specialist readers expect, and respond best to, a well-crafted, suspenseful story," Sarah Maya says of popular histories in *Thinking About History*.[3]

Family history places us somewhere between the disciplines of history and biography, disciplines that themselves are overlapping. Bearing in mind the differences up front helps us to understand not only our approach to research but also our approach to structuring and writing a narrative.

"Historians sift through masses of evidence in search of that which will advance their understanding of an event, an issue, a development in history. In that quest, people's roles and personalities are subordinate to the main agenda: what happened, when, and how. In biography, however, it's the other way around," says Nigel Hamilton in *How To Do Biography: A Primer*. "Biographical research, in other words, is impelled by curiosity about individual human nature, not the more impersonal forces of society and politics."[4]

Strictly speaking, family history is both history and biography. As a story of particular people bound together by a blood relation, biography's curiosity about individual human nature is at the heart of family history. As a story of a particular family's progress through time, it also is a history of what happened and when.

But family histories are more confined than either the typical biography or the typical history.

They're more confined than typical history because the focus is on one family. Consider the wealth of information on the Civil War. Now consider an American family with no member serving in the war and living in a place where no battles were fought. Obviously, the Civil War was on their minds and even influenced their lives, but as you construct their life story between 1861 and 1865, you might find yourself doing only a little research and writing on the details of America's deadliest war.

On the other hand, family stories are also more confined than typical biography, simply because there usually is so little material with which to work. The genealogist rightly sees the discovery of a birth certificate, a marriage license, and a death certificate as a triumph, but a biographer would hardly get beyond an opening line with that material alone.

So family story sits between history and biography, having narrower interest than the one and lesser material than the other. This fact has an important impact on both research and narrative. For example, a family story might lean heavily on more general history as a means of satisfying curiosity about an individual who can only be explained, in a second-hand way, by considering the recorded experiences of others in the same time, place, and circumstance. This is history put at the service of biography. Its value to our family story is measured only by how well it illuminates the lives and personalities of our ancestors.

These distinctions need to be understood, but they don't change those ingredients of a good story: engage, push forward, leave a lingering feeling.

ENGAGE READERS

Strong characters are the key to engaging readers. Strong characters have interesting personalities that engage their surroundings and circumstances in interesting ways. Their particular personalities—their virtues, their flaws, their values, their motivations, and their actions—make them compelling. You're unlikely to have an ancestor's personality described straightforwardly in the historic record (although there might be more out there than you realize). The motivation for a particular course of action, a land purchase for example, probably went unrecorded. However, you can look at the externals–the course of action itself and the surrounding circumstances–assess them thoughtfully, then assemble the facts to help make clear what a character's motivation probably was. Keep in mind that this is a narrative. Looking at the facts from all angles and toying with possibilities is essential to the process, but it's also something you're allowed to include in the narrative itself. Just use proper restraint and make sure readers can easily tell when you're speculating and when you're stating a demonstrated fact.

Bear in mind that a great personality sitting on the front porch being a great personality doesn't make a strong character. A strong character takes some kind of action. In particular, a strong character is engaged in conflict, some kind of conflict that is not only interesting but somehow shapes or typifies the history of your family. You'll find this kind of conflict in the push and pull of family migrations–the "why" of your family moves over the generations. You'll find it in the romances at the heart of the marriages on your charts, both the falling in love and the falling outs. You'll find it in any number of key moments that set a life, or rather a number of lives, on a particular path. A conflict might be a matter of life and death, it might be a matter of a broken heart, or it might seem inconsequential at the time with an importance that only reveals itself down the road. But if it is to engage readers, it has to be, in some way, momentous. Perhaps the conflict is critical to the life of the character, or particularly unusual and interesting, or so indicative of a person's life and personality as to be an analogy of the whole.

THE FALLEN FORTY-NINER

William Tattershall was the product of an old world. Not just of England, the place of his father's birth, but of his mother's Virginia, the Old Dominion itself, the place of his own birth and childhood.[5] But by 1849 in the shadow of the

Rocky Mountains, William was very much a man of someplace new, a place only just being born.

He was headed for California gold, having departed from Hannibal, Missouri, where he worked as a cooper and served as one of three founding elders of Hannibal Christian Church.[6] He left behind a wife and three children and was accompanied by his brother-in-law as part of a train of six ox wagons and two spring wagons.[7]

On 26 June of that year, William and two other men rode ahead of the wagon train to hunt for antelope. When one crossed not far from them, they all dismounted. One man shot and killed the antelope, but the gunfire scared the other man's horse as he pulled the trigger with the bridle still in his arm. The horse pulled him around, causing him to shoot William in the back.

"I am a dead man. O, my dear family," were his immediate words.

He died the next day and was buried near Apishapa River, "in a wild romantic valley surrounded by hills and overlooked by the Rocky Mountains where the foot of the white man may never have trodden before and where the Indian roams in search of game and the wolf prowls in search of his prey."[8]

Here is a momentous conflict. Man versus the wilderness. Risk versus reward. The responsibilities of home versus the prospect of wealth his family had never seen, nor would ever see otherwise. It becomes a matter of life and death, and all the worries for his family as he lay dying later realized.

What's more, it happens in the context of a major historical moment.

William's fatal journey also reveals a compelling character. A cooper with a wife and children in a little river town, leading an effort to start a new church, sounds like a man of some stability. And yet he headed down the Santa Fe Trail. He was a tradesman, a father, and a clergyman, but he was also an outdoorsman, a leader, a risk-taker. Which most drove him to head West: wealth or adventure?

The role of time and place is so important to engaging readers that the setting of your story should be considered a main character in its own right. Setting had a profound impact on the personalities and actions of our ancestors. And on a purely practical level, there will always be more information available on the setting of our ancestor's lives than there is on their actual lives.

You'll almost certainly want to sit down, take notes, and make lists of the characters and conflicts within your own family history. After all, if you're going to engage readers with compelling characters, you'll need to go about determining who they are in some sort of intentional way. However, you aren't going to actually engage readers until you've turned your notes and lists into a well-crafted narrative.

Think about the stories you've read (or watched or listened to) that have engaged you. Go back to them and consider

Figure 2. The last months of William Tattershall are described in a diary by the Rev. Benjamin Stevens, pictured in 1890, who accompanied him on the overland journey in 1849. Courtesy of the Hannibal Public Library.

what made them engaging. You'll need to cultivate a writing style that describes the facts of your story without getting distracted by explanations of where those facts came from. You'll need to cultivate a writing style that makes readers feel through concrete imagery rather than by telling them what to feel. You'll need to cultivate a writing style that uses descriptive language to create that imagery. Good writing–and a podcast or documentary will require good writing as much as a blog or a book–is the final key to engaging readers. It's an essential part of what makes characters and conflicts compelling.

PLOT YOUR COURSE

You've got interesting characters in meaningful conflict. Now their story needs to progress. In other words, you need a good plot.

Consider a traditional story. The plot unfolds with a premise introduced early, including the conflict. The story unfolds then resolves at the end. One effective part of this arrangement is that it provides readers with what they need to know early but the resolution remains a mystery, something readers want to learn, something that will keep them reading.

So a good plot deals with a conflict introduced early and an eventual resolution that entices readers to keep going to the end. In between, readers need to see progress toward that resolution throughout the story. Things need to be happening. Not just to the story, but to the characters as well. A family story is at its core about people, so the plot needs to reveal how the characters are changing, too. A good story doesn't just reveal how a conflict moves forward, it needs to show how the characters who are engaged in that conflict also are moving forward. How are they learning? How are they changing? How are they growing?

A good plot relies on a number of proven elements. Foreshadowing, for example, hints at where the story is going. Perhaps no story relies on foreshadowing more than Charlotte Brontë's *Jane Eyre*. For example, when Rochester proposes marriage to Jane, the reader is as much in the dark as Jane is about Rochester's mad wife locked on the third floor of Thornfield. But Brontë lets the reader know how the wedding is likely to end: "Before I left my bed in the morning, little Adèle came running in to tell me that the great horse-chestnut at the bottom of the orchard had been struck by lightning in the night, and half of it split away."[9]

Foreshadowing need not be so dramatic as an act of God. In *Ava's Man*, Rick Bragg's foreshadowing is more down to earth as he begins to tell the story of his family's origins as French Huguenots unwilling to back down even in the face of violent conflict.

"The beginning of their story goes way, way back, beyond them, even beyond the first Bundrum to drift here, to these green foothills that straddle the Alabama-Georgia border. In it, I found not only the beginnings of a family history but a clue to our character," he writes.[10]

There are a host of other elements you'll want to incorporate into your storytelling. Withhold information to create suspense in order to push the story forward. Look for good guys and bad guys, and research them thoroughly to fill them out, even if they aren't from your family tree. And focus particular attention on your opening and closing lines. The opening needs to instantly intrigue. The closing needs to resonate so that the story remains with readers after they've finished.

One strategy you might borrow from genealogy is the use of a timeline. Lining up key events chronologically will help you see your family story as it really unfolded. Key plot points are likely to emerge. The possibility of multiple perspectives, which often make a story more interesting, might present itself. With a timeline in hand, you'll be in the best position to decide if you want to tell your story chronologically or if there might be some better way to structure your family story. You'll spot where the story's premise best reveals itself–that's probably your introduction. You'll spot where the conflict resolves itself– that's probably your ending.

There's more to say on the subject of arranging, or outlining, your story, but that part comes in the final chapter.

HAVE A THEME: SOMETHING TO THINK ABOUT

Rich storytelling doesn't only describe plot and character well. It offers a theme, an overarching point or purpose that the story illustrates. Old-time family histories tended to botch this aspect of storytelling, with a theme something like: "The _____ family came from noble stock and continued to give noble witness to its nobility from noble generation to noble generation with a series of noble deeds."

Genealogy of the Grigsby Family in Part: Including a Brief Sketch of the Porter Family by William H. Grigsby, first published in 1878, opens with this:

> The Grigsbys are Anglo-Saxon. Goldsmith mentions their great number in England [In drama "She Stoops to Conquer."] Josiah, in 1794, in the House of Commons, seconded the motion of the celebrated Earl Gray, later prime minister of England, for a reform in the representation of Parliament. The English ancestors of our family came over to Virginia in about the year 1660, on the restoration of Charles II.; and were on the side of the Puritans, as Independents.[11]

It's hard to imagine Winney Grigsby, her daughter marrying a railroad worker in Hawkins County, Tennessee, in 1859, as part of such a distinguished lineage, her parents heading for the Appalachian hills about the time the Englishman Josiah Grigsby was seconding motions in the British Parliament.[12]

Fortunately, *Genealogy of the Grigsby Family in Part* quickly abandons its opening theme and instead presents an eight-page catalog of American Grigsbys, person by person and generation by generation, providing solid information that actually stands up to modern genealogical research better than the typical 19th-century family history. It becomes a helpful resource for an American family line. It never returns to its theme of Old World notability, but neither does it ever rise to the level of narrative storytelling. That's just as well. The family itself could never have kept up with William H. Grigsby's opening words. Most family history research quickly disavows even the noblest of families of this outdated theme. Our family histories, including that of the Virginia Grigsbys, are more interesting than that.

It's worth taking time to consider what your research has revealed. The more specific and profound your theme, the more likely it will lead to a unified and impactful family story. What is the character of your family? What are the traits and experiences that seem to repeat themselves from generation to generation? Maybe they were a particularly bold people. Maybe particularly industrious or particularly bright. If so, you probably have the beginnings of a theme for your family story.

The theme needs to be authentic, something discovered to be truly there on your family tree rather than something you artificially impose. Most family trees contain a wide variety of circumstances and character types. A common theme for many family stories would be, "Our family had a wide variety of characters doing a wide variety of things in a wide variety of places, but it all converged to make us who we are today." Even such a generalized theme can be helpful, as a starting point. For example, it might lead to the realization that the wide variety of characters and experiences from your family's past are still present in the current, varied generation. This could lead to some interesting storytelling–making jumps from people in the past to those alive today who seem to embody their spirit–if the current generation were amenable to such an approach. It would be an interesting way to preserve the oral history of the present generation alongside the documented history of a family's past.

While your family story typically will be about your ancestors rather than about yourself, there are times like the example above when the best theme puts you in the story. A lot of family histories published by trade publishers fall into this category, but you should resist the urge unless there is a good reason to do so. Bear in mind that family histories published by major publishers generally are written by established memoirists, historians, and biographers. English professor Alison Light, author of *Common People: In Pursuit of My Ancestors*, for example, had already published a biography of Virginia Woolf when the University of Chicago Press accepted her memoir of research into her own family's history. And Jeremy Hardy was a famous comedian when he published *My Family and Other Strangers: Adventures in Family History*.

    For the rest of us, generally speaking, we will serve as writer, not subject, but there are exceptions. Maybe you're an adopted child exploring the history of both your adoptive and biological families and finding interesting ways that you embody both. Maybe you've overcome some adversity only to discover that the struggle is a multi-generational one for your family. Incorporating your own experiences might help illuminate your family's past while also illuminating your own struggle. Be aware of the option, but cautious about using it.

    Developing a theme is a time for reflection. Once you have an impression of what your theme might be, you've only just begun. You need to keep pondering until the impression becomes something tangible. You should be able to state your theme in a sentence, and that sentence should immediately suggest possibilities and interest capable of driving a story.

    You have thirty-two fifth-great-grandparents, each from a family with its own tree and its own story. A family story will never be able to present a full account of your lineage's history. Reality dictates that you will have to narrow down the scope of your story. Genealogy, by definition, is a form of microhistory, but to tell a narrative story of your family's past requires scaling down even more, to a microhistory out of that microhistory. A family story is not a catalog of everything known about every ancestor.

    Typically, people focus on a particular family line to narrow their story, but theme will also help. You might, for example, turn the typical focus upside down and choose to write about all your thirty-two fifth-great-grandparents–them and them alone–choosing one generation for your focus instead of one family line. Who were they? What brought them together? What of their lives, if anything, became a part of your own character and the character of your more immediate family?

Spotting microhistories on your family tree can yield numerous opportunities for storytelling. For example, there are four generations of carpenters in the Wilmoth family. One built a bridge over the Hyco River where years earlier his parents had drowned while fording the stream when there was no bridge.[13] His son helped build a railroad line in Tennessee that was Destroyed during the Civil War and that his brother-in-law died trying to defend.[14] His grandson left a family farm in Kentucky to work as a carpenter in the city.[15] And his great-grandson became a carpenter for one of the Midwest's largest real estate firms at the dawn of the post-World War II building boom.[16]

The theme for the story of the Wilmoth carpenters might be: "The structures that a family of carpenters left behind over the course of two centuries not only became monuments to their skill and hard work but also to the times and places in which they lived."

Sometimes the themes aren't so optimistic. For example, alcoholism and abuse, where they exist, tend to exist generationally. However, telling these hard stories can offer future generations not only understanding, but also hope. Difficult themes like these require both forthrightness and compassion. Ideally, they focus on survival and redemption.

Ultimately, the theme of a family story should have relevance to present and future generations as well as to the past.

"I think that we all have a need to find out where we came from, and invariably there is some history, some truth, that explains who we are to our own satisfaction. Some of us reject it and make a different path for ourselves. And some of us embrace these notions and put them on display for everyone to see," Julie Klam writes in *The Almost Legendary Morris Sisters: A True Story of Family Fiction*.[17]

Characters, plot, theme. These are the key elements of good storytelling, the means to engaging readers, pushing them forward, and leaving them with something after they've finished. Fiction writers get to create these elements from their imaginations, but telling your particular family story requires discovering these elements from your own history. This means researching with storytelling in mind. No longer are you looking at records just to discover birth, marriage, and death. Now, you're looking for those key elements of storytelling. That requires adding new approaches to your research.

---

[3] Sarah Maza, *Thinking About History* (Chicago: University of Chicago Press, 2017), 126.

[4] Nigel Hamilton, *How To Do Biography: A Primer* (Cambridge: Harvard University Press, 2008), 64-66.

[5] The 1850 U.S. census enumerated William Tattershall's parents in Hamilton County, Ohio, where William married in 1832 and was himself enumerated in 1840.

[6] R.I. Holcombe *History of Marion County, Missouri: Written and Compiled from the Most Authentic Official and Private Sources. Including a History of Its Townships, Towns, and Villages, Together with a Condensed History of Missouri; the City of St. Louis, a Reliable and Detailed History of Marion County–Its Pioneer Record, War History, Resources, Biographical Sketches and Portraits of Prominent Citizens; General and Local Statistics of Great Value ... and Reminiscences, Grave, Tragic and Humorous* (St. Louis: E.F. Perkins, 1884), 981.

[7] J.D. Dawson, "Obituary: Bro. William Tattershall," *Millennial Harbinger* series III, volume VI, no. XI (November 1849), 657. Benjamin Stevens, *1849 Journal of Overland Trip to California*, 20 April 1849, John Lewis RoBards Papers, State Historical Society of Missouri.

[8] *1849 Journal of Overland Trip to California*, entries for June 1849.

[9] Charlotte Brontë, *Jane Eyre* (New York: J.M. Dent & Sons, 1922): 255.

[10] Rick Bragg, *Ava's Man* (New York: Vintage Books, 2001): 26.

[11] W.H. Grigsby, *Genealogy of the Grigsby Family in Part: Including a Brief Sketch of the Porter Family* (Chicago: R.H. McCormick, 1905, republished), 1.

[12] The 1850 U.S. census enumerated Mary Frances Smith in the Hawkins County, Tennessee, household of William and Winney Grigsby Smith nine years before her Hawkins County marriage to John Wilmoth.

[13] Walter James Wilmoth, *Wilmoths in America from 1623-2009* (Heiskell: W.J. Wilmoth, 2009), 38.
[14] *Wilmoths in America*, 50. Leland L. Smith, editor, *A Smith in Service: Diaries of Calvin Morgan Smith 1847-1864* (Rogersville: Hawkins County Genealogical & Historical Society, 2000), 96.
[15] *Caron's Directory of the City of Louisville* (Louisville: Caron Directory Co., 1907), 1593.
[16] *Williams' Newport City Directory* (Cincinnati: Williams Directory Co., 1944), 328.
[17] Julie Klam, *The Almost Legendary Morris Sisters: A True Story of Family Fiction* (New York: Riverbend Books, 2021), 237.

Chapter Two
The Stuff

Genealogy attempts to determine facts about vital events–birth, marriage, and death–in order to establish reliable family lineages. It has its own standards regarding sources and conclusions, but those standards draw primarily from the legal profession. After all, drawing genealogical conclusions requires proving a case.

However, your family story will need to draw more from the fields of history and biography. These fields are more focused on interpreting data. You might be correct in saying they're more speculative with records than a lawyer would be, but that would be missing the most important point. A historian or biographer's interpretation is not meant to be a flight of fancy. Where a lawyer tends to distill information in a record to its provable facts, historians and biographers seek to deepen knowledge of a record through their interpretation. For example, knowing the ins and outs of particular social stratifications–such as rich and poor, man and woman, or black and white–can deepen understanding of a record that on the surface simply looks like a straightforward legal transaction. For historians and biographers, understanding the context surrounding a record is essential. None of this is new to the seasoned genealogist, but it becomes more essential when telling your family story. Understanding context ranges from big-picture stuff like world events to the deeply personal like an individual's past struggles.

As such, researching your family story will involve deepening your interaction with historic records. When filling out my family tree, the main information I wanted from my great-grandparents' divorce record was the divorce date. When I took a closer look, I was able to verify their marriage date and their children as well, which was nice. But when writing my family story, the depositions in my great-grandparents' divorce provided far more than names and dates. It told the whole story of their marriage from the mouths of the ancestors themselves. It revealed a marriage that turned bitter early on, even though it lasted thirty-four years. Now, I can interpret the twenty-year gap between their only two children in a way that is both fact-based and illuminating.

In other words, records you're already relying on for vital events also contain details of value to your family story. Military registrations over the course of American history are nice as backup sources for things like birth dates, but where else will you routinely find a physical description of your ancestors? It's interesting to know, for example, that since at least the 19th century, the men in my family have typically come in one of two sizes: five-foot-seven-inches tall and 140 pounds or five-foot-eleven-inches tall and 140 pounds. (I'm the former, plus a few pounds.)

Family story research will sometimes move to the forefront records that generally play a more secondary role in genealogy. They lack the authority of birth, marriage, and death certificates when it comes to determining vital events, but they also present an abundance of tales that can feed your family story and provide leads for further research.

ORAL HISTORY

The author Harriette Simpson Arnow grew up in the early twentieth century with family history shared through storytelling, so much so that she opened *Seedtime on the Cumberland* by telling the story of "Granpa" fording a flooded Brandywine Creek to join Count Pulaski in the fight for American independence as if she were there watching it happen in the eighteenth century.

"Which Granpa? How many greats back? I never asked. In time I learned his name was Thomas Merritt. He was only one of many grandfathers and grandmothers, uncles and aunts, their kith, kin, and enemies, as well as many animals, both wild and domestic, who came to our house, often as now in winter when the lamps were lighted, and the black and ugly wood burning stove a sister had named Hirschevogel filled the room with heat and a pleasant roaring," she writes.[18]

If your family told such stories, write them down. Talk to other family members and compare how they remember the details. Then go to the historic record and see what can be verified and what can be added.

But even if your family didn't share stories from generations ago, you can start now with those still living. Talk to family members, especially the older ones, and record their memories. To give it its full value, do so systematically. This means:

• Conduct a structured, well-researched interview. Prepare beforehand–know what you want to get from the interview and have a list of questions to start with.

• Use a controlled, recorded interview setting. Record the interview–video, ideally–with good lighting, good sound insulation, and no distractions.

• Focus on first-hand information. This should be the focus, although family lore has its value, too.

• Ask follow-up questions that seek depth and detail. A conversational approach might draw out better information, but be sure to let your subject do most of the talking, uninterrupted.

• Use high-quality recording equipment. Test the equipment to make sure you know how it works and that you know how to get the quality you want.

• Process recordings in a way that enhances quality and preservation of files. You'll want to use backup copies and offsite drives to make sure you don't lose something irreplaceable.

• Make them available. Decide how and with whom you're going to share what you've collected.[19]

Chances are, by collecting your family's oral history, you'll be adding something new to the larger body of collected oral histories. There are now so many oral histories, it's in your interest to check to see if your family–or the time and place you're researching–is represented in any of the many public oral history collections out there. The Oral History Association (oralhistory.org) has a list of some of the larger repositories, but as with all your research, you'll also want to touch base with local public libraries and historical societies for the best leads at ground level.

PERSONAL LETTERS AND DIARIES

We often have a preconceived image of how people behaved in the past. Maybe it's the old portraits and photos with not a smile to be seen, but I tend to imagine people as more formal and more stoic. But when I come across personal letters and diaries in my family history, they typically reveal greater humor, quirkier personalities, and stronger depth of emotion than my preconceived image would have allowed. Lots of people wrote letters, but few of those letters survive. Fewer people kept diaries. So when we find them, they're a treasure.

Calvin Morgan Smith was a farmer, a teacher, and a soldier. He also was a diarist. Six of his diaries cover his military service, ranging from a brief stint in the Mexican-American War in 1847 to his penultimate campaign in the Civil War in 1864. Amid these wartime chronicles is the diary of a month-long flatboat journey down the Holston River to sell a store of accumulated goods including kraut, cider, apples, pickles, apple butter, and turnips. This diary could easily be used as the basis for the narrative of an Appalachian odyssey, with an abundance of characters, places, and observations as a starting point (and all requiring their own research). The diary reveals a man entirely at ease with his surroundings, both the landscape and the array of people he met. Timekeeping itself proves poetic, marked as it was by such things as "moon down" and "as the morning star arose." The passing of the steamboat *Elk* prompted an especially wistful response:

> This morning reminded me of busy spring, the crowing of the roosters, singing of the old hens, the chirping of the feathered tribe in general brought to mind the recollections of the past. The deep water wafted us slowly on in silent submission, upon whose bosom the steam boats ride in safety. Seated as I am I hear the distant

scraping of some boat on its downward passage. But, Oh, listen! She is going to land opposite a little town one mile from the river. How she sounds her horn! She is highly steamed, but she has now landed [...] no one from town yet. She blows again yet louder, making the welkin ring again. How she is loaded and here she comes, just room to pass. Great and powerful are the works of men![20]

Smith's diaries were published by the Hawkins County Genealogical & Historical Society, a testament to the work done at the local level. Personal papers might be found at large statewide and national repositories, such as special collection libraries at colleges and universities, or they might be kept locally, even in personal hands. All my success stories with letters, diaries, and memoirs originated through online engagement with other genealogists who already had discovered the material. When you hear of something, get the details and get to the source, preferably the original.

NEWSPAPERS

Historians have traditionally avoided newspapers as a primary source, in spite of journalism's claim they are "the first draft of history." Reporters might be writing on the day of an event based on interviews with first-hand witnesses, but concerns about misquotes, partisanship, and breezy incompleteness typically temper the historian's enthusiasm. Nevertheless, historic newspapers provide an abundance of information across time and place. Every week, and increasingly every day as the 19th century progressed, newspapers printed stories from around the world and around the corner. By the later half of that century, social calls, local entertainment, the police blotter, and detailed obituaries all were finding a place in local papers. In some cases, the official documents recording the events are now lost. In others, the events weren't recorded anywhere else in the first place. Ignore newspapers as a source, however, and you'll never know that gold-bearing quartz was said to have been found late summer 1897 near Reelfoot Lake at the Kentucky-Tennessee state line.[21] You'll never know of the vivacious time had at Miss Dora Salyers' candy party, nor of the falling out between Isaac Rector and Hays Smith, in which a good many shots were fired but no one hurt, nor of the petty thief who stole a tray of shoes from the traveling salesman B.F. Weller only to find the shoes were all for the same foot.[22]

There are any number of sources for historical newspapers, digitized and searchable. A paid subscription is needed for some, like Newspapers.com, NewsBank, NewspaperArchive, and ProQuest. There are also great free sources, led by the Library of Congress's *Chronicling America* (chroniclingamerica.loc.gov) but also ranging from statewide sources like the Colorado Historic Newspapers Collection to individual newspapers like the *Mount Vernon Signal*, digitized and archived by the Rockcastle County Public Library in Mount Vernon, Kentucky (home of Miss Dora Salyers' candy party).

There's even more to find in real life. Local public libraries can generally be relied on to have a good collection of their historical local newspapers. However, you'll have to approach these collections, usually on microfilm, differently from online collections. "When to look" becomes as important as "where to look." But the ability to narrow down a timeframe and a willingness to spend some time perusing pages will often bring you to what you're looking for. I found detailed coverage of a second-great uncle's escape from the Lexington, Kentucky, jail in 1874–an escape that "for coolness is rarely equalled"–in spite of the fact the coverage never mentioned his name. I simply knew the month of his larceny conviction eighty miles north of

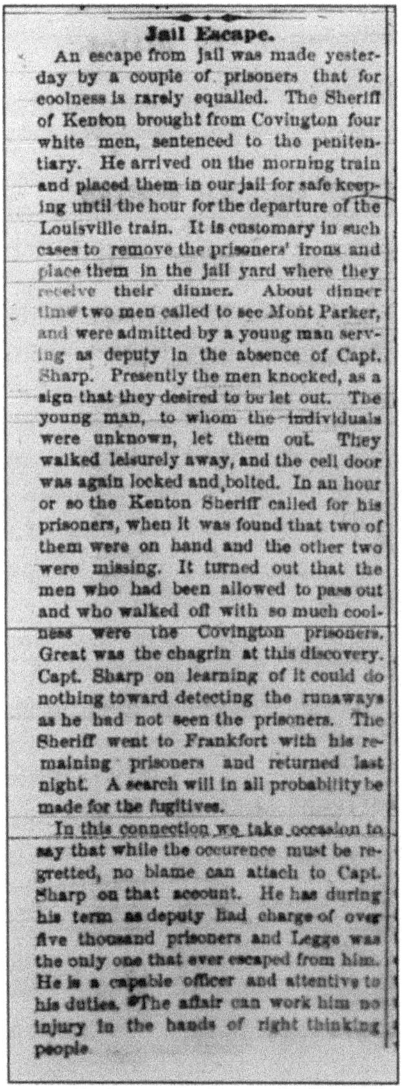

Jail Escape.

An escape from jail was made yesterday by a couple of prisoners that for coolness is rarely equalled. The Sheriff of Kenton brought from Covington four white men, sentenced to the penitentiary. He arrived on the morning train and placed them in our jail for safe keeping until the hour for the departure of the Louisville train. It is customary in such cases to remove the prisoners' irons and place them in the jail yard where they receive their dinner. About dinner time two men called to see Mont Parker, and were admitted by a young man serving as deputy in the absence of Capt. Sharp. Presently the men knocked, as a sign that they desired to be let out. The young man, to whom the individuals were unknown, let them out. They walked leisurely away, and the cell door was again locked and bolted. In an hour or so the Kenton Sheriff called for his prisoners, when it was found that two of them were on hand and the other two were missing. It turned out that the men who had been allowed to pass out and who walked off with so much coolness were the Covington prisoners. Great was the chagrin at this discovery. Capt. Sharp on learning of it could do nothing toward detecting the runaways as he had not seen the prisoners. The Sheriff went to Frankfort with his remaining prisoners and returned last night. A search will in all probability be made for the fugitives.

In this connection we take occasion to say that while the occurence must be regretted, no blame can attach to Capt. Sharp on that account. He has during his term as deputy had charge of over five thousand prisoners and Legge was the only one that ever escaped from him. He is a capable officer and attentive to his duties. The affair can work him no injury in the hands of right thinking people.

Figure 3. Benjamin Tattershall's clever escape from the Lexington jail was considered newsworthy by the Daily Lexington Press, *but coverage neglected to include his name. Courtesy of the Lexington Public Library.*

there and the fact that he escaped in Lexington while being transported to the state penitentiary in nearby Frankfort.[23]

LAWSUITS

From a storytelling perspective, court trials present a narrative as dramatically as any stage play or television drama, which is why they've so often been made into stage plays and television dramas. Go back in time far enough, and a transcript probably won't exist for the trial your ancestor was party to, but the lawsuit's file very well might. It will provide at least some of the drama of a trial.

Americans have been a litigious people since colonial times, so there is an abundance of material. Lawsuits typically involve disputes about money owed, but they can be about almost anything that would pit one party against another. In court records, you'll learn about divorces, land disputes, inheritance squabbles, contract disagreements, and personal injuries and grievances. Remember: a good story involves conflict, and lawsuits are all about conflict.

What's more, court records often take on the tone of a narrative. To argue a specific complaint requires providing background, identifying the parties, and explaining the problem in some detail. A file might also include transcripts of depositions or interviews of the parties conducted prior to a trial, providing testimony in the witnesses' own words.

Historic lawsuits are often centrally kept in state archives, although the local court clerk might hold onto them instead, in some cases. You'll need to consult indexes to see if your ancestor shows up, get a case number, then get the actual file. By the late 19th century, some newspapers had begun to regularly list lawsuits filed in their local courts, so they're a good source as well. And if for some reason a lawsuit listed in a newspaper isn't indexed, you'll have some idea of the timing and what box of old files to thumb through.

It's worthwhile to look at any lawsuit involving your ancestors in any capacity. In 1821, John McGeath sued his brother-in-law John H. Cassaday in Frederick County, Virginia, for selling timber from land owned by McGeath's deceased father. McGeath argued that his father's will did not allow Cassaday to profit from the land, but Cassaday argued that it was allowed because he only sold timber that already had fallen to the ground. The lawsuit had nothing to do with my ancestors except that Cassaday sold the timber to a road crew that included Thomas Tattershall, my fourth-great grandfather. All the road crew members were deposed, but McGeath argued that Tattershall's testimony should be struck because he was a British citizen and therefore shouldn't have been permitted on the road crew in the first place.[24] This little dispute within the lawsuit provides an interesting coda to the story of Thomas Tattershall's declaration of intent to become a U.S. citizen nine years earlier.

CENTENNIAL HISTORIES

On 2 March 1876, the United States Senate passed a joint resolution of Congress recommending that counties and towns across America deliver a historical sketch of their communities as part of their celebration of the Centennial of national independence the following Fourth of July, and to file a printed version of that sketch both locally and at the Library of Congress.[25] The resolution prompted a spree of published local histories.

Only to varying degrees do these local histories meet the standard of accurate history and engaging narrative. They contain a wealth of information but a dearth of citation, and for the most part, they make for dry reading. However, having been researched and written in the 19th century, they contain great detail on the early days of the communities that made up America, with some of that detail drawn from first-hand recollection.

These histories also only met the Centennial deadline to varying degrees. Many of them were written years after 1876. Reese Kendall was working for the *Cincinnati Tribune* seventeen years after the Centennial when he published memories of early life in Green Township, where he had been born in 1829.[26]

Kendall's *Pioneer Annals of Greene Township* is sparse on traditional history, although his demarcation of the term *pioneer*—fireplace cooking—is elegant and insightful. The availability of Cincinnati industrialist William Resor's new stove in 1839 becomes a clean, legitimate line that matches well with Kendall's other marks of the pioneer era: log cabins and the local militia system.[27] But Kendall's real focus is on personal recollections—his own and those of other old-timers still around in the 1890s. The result is nothing the average reader would ever have waiting on his nightstand except as a cure for insomnia, but it is a boon for scores of family lines that trace their way through this particular patch of farms and mills and taverns just northwest of Cincinnati. The heart of the book is a systematic list of everything Kendall remembers about everyone who lived in Green, organized alphabetically by name.

Only because of Kendall do I know that my first cousin five times removed was "Full of fun, always jolly" and "played the violin for all festivities," which is especially interesting since that cousin's father was excommunicated from the Methodist Church for playing the fiddle and reinstated only because he claimed he just played the instrument to demonstrate it to a man to whom he was selling it.[28] Only because of Kendall do I know that my third-great-grandfather had significant woods south of his small farm, in which Kendall and a friend got lost as boys.[29] Only because of Kendall do I know that my fifth-great-grandmother lived in a brick house that looked very old by 1843.

"She was the lady of whom we bought corn in 1844 and who said 'I told the boys to raise some 'cow corn', plant thick to make nubbins, but it's most all that kind!' A mild, lovable woman," he wrote of her.[30]

Nine years before Kendall started writing down his memories of Green Township, a jury in Cincinnati returned a lesser verdict of manslaughter in a case of unquestioned, premeditated murder. It sparked outrage and riots. When they had ended, more than fifty people were dead and the Hamilton County courthouse was destroyed. Today, early 19th-century marriage licenses and other Hamilton County records that genealogists work with are actually reconstructions that clerks did their best to assemble after the riots had done their damage. There are major gaps in the record and missing pieces on the reconstructions.[31] Although genealogy experts rightly warn against placing too much trust in Centennial local histories, *Pioneer Annals of Greene Township* provides not only a host of colorful details, but in several cases it also provides the best evidence of who married whom, their occupations, and where they lived.

So the value of these local histories should not be ignored, especially for storytelling. When moving from family tree to family story, having a direct quote from a pioneer ancestor is a treasure, even if it is about something as insignificant as her advice on planting field corn. Thanks to Kendall, we catch a glimpse of a widow who had raised fifteen children and buried two more. There she is, late in life, standing outside her dilapidated brick house, mild and lovable to the boys of the neighborhood, teaching them something of what she learned as a pioneer and teasing them for taking her advice a little too far. It's a brief, simple moment, but a powerful glimpse into the past.

There are a wealth of Centennial histories to be found online, at sites like Archive.org and Google Books. And what isn't online is typically on the shelves of the public library in the community about which the Centennial history was written.

All these sources are familiar to genealogists, but when it comes to birth, marriage, and death, they're not definitive sources. We take extra care to scrutinize their reliability and verify any asserted facts against documents that have more official status. That's good advice for using them for your family story as well. But your questions won't just have to do with determining reliability of the facts. Like the historian and biographer, you'll need to interpret the documents. Who wrote it and why? What unintentional biases influenced it? What intentional biases and agendas influenced it? Is there a subtext that reveals hidden meanings? What perspectives are missing from it, and can those perspectives be found elsewhere? What does it really contribute to the story you want to tell?

AFFECTIVE HISTORY

One way to understand your ancestors' history is to relive it in the form of re-enactment. "Affective history," as it's known, uses living history experiences to better understand the past. Civil War re-enactors, for example, go to great lengths to achieve authenticity in large part to feel a connection to a past event, as a way to understand it and to honor those who truly lived it. In many cases, re-enactors use a specific person, often an ancestor, as a model when creating their uniforms and assembling their gear.

However, your re-enactment need not be as elaborate as that. If you want to understand a great-great grandmother who quilted, you might join a quilting bee. If you want to understand ancestors who homesteaded, you might try growing at least a little of your own food or raising your own chickens. If you want to understand a grandfather who was a miner, you might go down into a coal mine.

"My urge was to go directly to the original materials–and most especially to the *places*–for myself, and risk the numerous details that I might consequently (and did on occasions) get wrong," Percy Shelley biographer Richard Holmes wrote of his decision to retrace Shelley's footsteps in Italy 165 years later.[32]

This urge drove Holmes eventually to the garden of Casa Bertini, where Shelley had spent time translating Plato's *Symposium* in the summer of 1818.

"I walked into the grove and turned back, seeing in one flash what Shelley saw as he looked up from his table, with his Greek lexicon and his Marcello Ficino and his scattered paragraphs of Plato. The light was fading and there was a smell of damp leaves that reminded me of England," Holmes observed.[33]

Experimental archaeology, in which archaeologists and anthropologists recreate methods of past living and working, is something of a peer to affective history. However, they have been received differently within their respective academic fields. The difference is worth considering because it helps the storyteller better understand how to incorporate the personal experiences of re-enactment into a family history narrative.

Affective history has been met with skepticism by many academic historians because so much of its purpose is emotional connection. In fact, your emotional experience to a re-enactment in no way determines how an ancestor felt going through that original moment. At best, it only suggests how an ancestor might have felt.

On the other hand, experimental archaeology seeks to better understand how certain activities worked in a particular time and place by using the same methods and resources to

[19] Barbara W. Sommer and Mary Kay Quinlan, *The Oral History Manual* (Lanham: AltaMira Press, 2009), 1.

[20] Smith, *A Smith in Service: Diaries of Calvin Morgan Smith 1847-1864*, 32-33.

[21] *Mount Vernon Signal*, 17 September 1897, 1.

[22] Items from *Mount Vernon Signal*: 11 December 1896, 2; 22 January 1897, 2; 22 January 1897, 2.

[23] "Escape from Jail," *Daily Lexington Press*, 18 February 1874, 4.

[24] Frederick County, Virginia, Chancery Court no. 1821-162, John McGeath et al. vs. John H. Cassaday, 1 October 1821, Library of Virginia.

[25] "Centennial Celebration," *Congressional Record* 4, 2 March 1876, 1402.

[26] *Portrait and Biographical Record of Western Oregon: Containing Original Sketches of Many Well Known Citizens of the Past and Present* (Chicago: Chapman Publishing Co., 1904), 971-972.

[27] Reese P. Kendall, *Pioneer Annals of Greene Township: Hamilton County, Ohio* (San Jose: Geo. F. Degelman, 1905), 8.

[28] Kendall, *Pioneer Annals of Greene Township*, 43. *Autobiography of Daniel Isgrig*, 90.

[29] Kendall, *Pioneer Annals of Greene Township*, 39.

[30] Kendall, *Pioneer Annals of Greene Township*, 43.

[31] Steven McQuillin, "History of Records," Hamilton County Probate Court, https://www.probatect.org/about/history-of-records.

[32] Richard Holmes, *Footsteps: Adventures of a Romantic Biographer* (New York: Elizabeth Sifton Books-Viking, 1985), 136.

[33] *ibid.*, 147-148.

[34] John Coles, *Experimental Archaeology* (London: Academic Press, 1979), 57-63.

Chapter Three
Puzzle Pieces

Belle Brezing was a famous madam even before she appeared in *Gone With the Wind* as the character Belle Watling, the Atlanta prostitute who provides a phony alibi for Scarlett's husband after a nighttime raid. Brezing was much talked about in her hometown, to the point that her public persona is as much a part of her story as the life she actually lived. Some of that persona defies belief, like the rumor that she convinced a syndicate of businessmen to buy the local water company when her long-time lover was at risk of losing his job there due to his relationship with her.

You'll find mention of the rumor among oral histories about the heyday of her three-story, eighteen-bedroom brothel in Lexington, Kentucky.[35] But there isn't likely to be any historic record that would verify or refute such a rumor in any kind of direct, reliable way. The rumor offers a puzzle to the researcher: Is the story fact or fiction?

Don't overlook the term *puzzle*. A puzzle is made up of pieces, and while there's nothing to directly answer the question about the veracity of the rumor, the rumor itself asserts a number of things that can be verified or refuted. They're pieces to the puzzle. The goal is to put them together in the right way. Here are some of them:

• Billy Mabon was well known to be Belle Brezing's longtime lover and to have taken up residence with her in her brothel. One of his gifts to her–the book *Lucille* by Owen Meredith, which he inscribed, "From Will to Kitten March 4th 1888"–is still kept at the University of Kentucky's Margaret I. King Library.[36]

• C.H. Stoll, leader of the syndicate that purchased Lexington Water Works Co., is known to have been one of Brezing's customers.[37]

• When the local newspaper reported the sale, it made a point to mention that Mabon would keep his job as bookkeeper.[38]

So the historic record verifies what details about the rumor are verifiable. What's more, the context of those details also bolsters the rumor:

- Brezing was a woman of means and influence. Her longtime patron was a bank president who owned a Philadelphia newspaper and a paper mill. In politics, he supported the successful presidential campaign of his close personal friend Grover Cleveland.[39] Her local connections were even stronger. She had the pull to make the water company sale happen.
- The local press was in the habit of covering Brezing with varying degrees of subtlety. For example, years after her death, a family lawsuit attempting to disinherit the widow of Judge John J. Riley was big news in town largely because the widow was one of Brezing's old prostitutes. The newspaper covered the trial closely, but never mentioned the reason

Figure 4. Belle Brezing sits among the finery in her private parlor at her famous sporting house for men. Courtesy of University of Kentucky Special Collections.

everybody in town was talking about it.[40] Likewise, mention of Mabon in the water company article, without any explanation as to why his fate in particular was worth mentioning, might have been a nod to what everybody knew was at the heart of the sale.

None of this proves the rumor true. So should it be omitted from the story of this woman's rise to fame, wealth, and even power? Absolutely not. To tell the story, you might spend a little time describing the pros and cons of the rumor's veracity, but only a little time. Mainly, you would assemble the facts, tell the story, and let readers decide for themselves.

This is just one example of a story never directly told that can nevertheless be assembled by putting together the puzzle pieces, the facts from their various sources as well as the context of the whole thing. This is similar to the work we do as genealogists when direct evidence doesn't provide an answer about birth, marriage, or death. We put together all the pieces and see if they provide a clearer picture.

Go back to your timeline. This chronological assembly of events will help you analyze all the information you have, even if it doesn't dictate the order that your narrative takes. However, a timeline of your ancestors' lives won't be enough. You need to include details from the lives of other characters–C.H. Stoll, for example–as well as key events happening around them at the time. You're assembling for narrative storytelling. It's time to think like a historian and a biographer, and those extra puzzle pieces might have important answers on them. On top of that, telling a story from multiple perspectives can make for a better story.

WESTWARD BOUND, BUT WHY?

In the early decades of the 1800s, Thomas Tattershall was working as a shoemaker in Alexandria, a city within the District of Columbia at that time. He had been in the city since at least 1803, when he married Nancy Boyd, but he only declared his intention of becoming a U.S. citizen on 18 July 1812.[41] On 16 March 1813, a young Gabriel Bradley was bound to Tattershall to learn the art of a boot and shoe maker. However, the boy was bound to another Alexandria shoemaker on 22 October 1814.[42] The next record of Tattershall comes nearly six years later in the *Genius of Liberty*, a newspaper in Loudoun County, Virginia:

> THOMAS TATTERSHALL,
> Boot and Shoe Maker,
> RESPECTFULLY informs the gentlemen and ladies of Waterford, that he has
> commenced the above business, one door below Dulaney's tavern, and nearly
> opposite Mr. David Shawen's store, where he will carry it on in all its variety,
> with neatness, accuracy, and dispatch. Those who may favour him with their
> custom may rely upon the strictest punctuality; and all orders will be strictly
> attended to.
> March 7, 1820.—8 3t.[43]

Absent more information, this collection of facts might simply catalog the beginning of the family's migration away from the Eastern Seaboard, just another example of the massive westward pull exerted on the American population in the early 19th century. However, a little knowledge of U.S. history raises immediate questions, and a little bit of additional research provides an entirely different explanation.

America declared war on Great Britain on 18 June 1812, precisely one month before Tattershall declared his intention of becoming a citizen. Under a fourteen-year-old law, he and twelve thousand other British subjects in the United States found themselves "liable to be apprehended, restrained, secured, and removed." The U.S. government then required British aliens to report to U.S. marshals "the persons composing their families, the places of their residence and their occupations or pursuits, and whether, and at what time, they have made the application to the courts required by law, as preparatory to their naturalization."[44]

These events just across the Potomac River almost certainly precipitated Tattershall's appearance at the Arlington courthouse to declare his intention to become a citizen. He remained in Alexandria during the first couple years of the War of 1812, taking on an apprentice in 1813, but by October 1814 his apprentice had found someone new to work for. What happened?

The burning of Washington happened.

Five days after the burning of Washington, on 29 August 1814, the British occupied Alexandria, with an agreement between local leaders that avoided the destruction of their city. By the time British ships arrived there, the city was largely empty.[45] There's a good chance Tattershall and his family had already left, but the evidence suggests it wasn't of his own free will.

Figure 5. The former shoemaking shop of Thomas Tattershall in Waterford, Virginia, pictured in the center from a photograph taken in 1937. Courtesy of the Waterford Foundation.

Waterford, Virginia, where Tattershall would commence business as a boot and shoe maker in 1820, is almost precisely forty miles upstream from Alexandria. During the War of 1812, British aliens living in port cities that might be a target of invasion were required to relocate at least forty miles upstream.[46] Tattershall probably left Alexandria sometime in the summer of 1814, but he only went as far as the law required.

Figure 6. The former shoemaking shop of Thomas Tattershall, behind poles, in Waterford, Virginia, today. Courtesy of the Waterford Foundation.

Although records in the National Archives show registered aliens from every state, there are none registered in the District of Columbia.[47] Given the timing of Tattershall's appearance in court, it seems likely he, at least, was registered in the district. However, the record apparently was lost or might likely have been destroyed two years later during the burning of Washington. And thanks to McGeath vs. Cassaday, we know that Tattershall never followed through on his declaration of intent.

In genealogy, descriptions of certainty help increase the accuracy of our stated conclusions (e.g., John Wooley Isgrigg *probably* married Susanna Shotts about 1814 in Hamilton County, Ohio). The same distinctions help with the accuracy of our family stories. They allow us to include important story points without overstating what we know. What's more, family lore and community rumor might find a relevant place in narrative storytelling even if their truth can't be verified. If you were to decide the rumor that Brezing and the purchase of Lexington Water Works wasn't true, for example, you might still include it as an example of her image and reputation in her own hometown.

Like countless genealogists, Nigel Hamilton, author of *How To Do Biography*, also extols the value of a timeline. He further encourages biographers to consider Shakespeare's "Seven Ages of Man" (from *As You Like It*) as a way to gain a complete picture of a life. Hamilton labels these ages as: childhood, education, relationships, apprenticeship, success, aging, and the end.[48] Even when your interest is in one specific moment of a person's life, you would do well to consider that whole life in all its phases.

Often in family history, there are key moments you know happened, but you know very little about what those moments were like. This is one place where the larger history and even other biographies can help. They can provide parallel descriptors and details about what an ancestor might have experienced.

John Roberts departed Cornwall on 9 April 1847 and sailed to Quebec on the ship *Clio*. He kept an account of his trip with such entries as:

> April 18 Sunday Morning–I woke but very unwell. I had a little grual for breakfast, & after breakfast (it been Sunday) I begun to think about the chapple & the people that sat in their different seats & about my Fathers House & if I was home what a good dinner I could make, but all the thinking was of no use. I got out of bed, dressed & went on deck but the weather was very rough & I was so unwell I was obliged to go to bed again & in the night I woke & heard the captain calling take that sail & furl the others & there was so much sea I was afraid she would turn over.[49]

The diary of Roberts' transatlantic voyage in steerage documents the seasickness, the food, the disease and death, the homesickness, as well as the more comforting moments of the journey. David and Catherine Hoban left Liverpool three years later on the *U.S.S. Oxford*. A different ship and a different journey, lives entirely unconnected to John Roberts. But the family story of the Hobans can benefit from Roberts' diary, inasmuch as it presents a typical Atlantic crossing for the time. Understanding the limits of the parallel is important. For example, crossing much earlier would have been far more crowded and in conditions far more brutal, due to looser regulation. But in 1850 on the *Oxford*, there's every reason to think the experience of the Hobans was similar to that of John Roberts three years earlier on the *Clio*.

This bigger picture of history allows us to understand our particular family story, especially when the details of our own story are lacking.

For Alison Light, in *Common People*, the social history of Great Britain provided essential insight that explained her ancestors' migrations and life changes. Without an understanding of the constantly-shifting ground for workers during 19th-century industrialism, she would have been left wondering why her ancestors made the moves they made across southern England.

"Unless it is to be simply a catalogue of names, the history of a family is impossible to fathom without coming up for air and scanning the wider horizon," she writes.[50]

---

[35] Joe Keith, interview with Joe Jordan, 10 February 1956, Buddy Thompson Papers, File 38-8, University of Kentucky Special Collections.

[36] Inscribed book, Buddy Thomas Papers.

[37] William Townsend, *The Most Orderly of Disorderly Houses* (Lexington: privately printed, 1966), 4-6.

[38] "Water Works: Formally Passes into Control of the New Local Syndicate: Payment of $230,000 in Cash Completes the Important Transaction: C.H. Stoll the New President," *Lexington Leader*, 13 November 1904, section 2, 1.

[39] Townsend, *The Most Orderly of Disorderly Houses*, 6.

[40] "Evidence of Early Marriage Introduced in Contest of Will," *Lexington Leader*, 1 March 1951, 1.

[41] Circuit Court of Alexandria County, 18 July 1812, unpaginated, microfilm 00578, Alexandria (Virginia) Library.

[42] T. Michael Miller, *Portrait of a Town: Alexandria: District of Columbia [Virginia] 1820-1830* (Bowie: Heritage Books, 1995), 419.

[43] "Thomas Tattershall, Boot and Shoe Maker," *Genius of Liberty* (Leesburg, Virginia), 7 March 1820, 3.

[44] Kenneth Scott, editor, *British Aliens in the United States During the War of 1812* (Baltimore: Genealogical Publishing Co., 1979), v-vii.

[45] Ted Pulliam, *Alexandria and the War of 1812: A Series of Articles Telling How Alexandrians Were Affected 200 Years Ago by the War of 1812* (Alexandria: Alexandria Archeology Publications, 2014), 22-25.

[46] Scott, *British Aliens in the United States During the War of 1812*, vii.

[47] *Ibid*. The one Alexandria resident whose registration survives lived in the portion of the city still located in Fairfax County, Virginia.

[48] Hamilton, *How To Do Biography: A Primer*, 99-101.

[49] Edwin C. Guillet, *The Great Migration: The Atlantic Crossing by Sailing-Ship 1770-1860* (Toronto: University of Toronto Press, 1963), 11 (supplement).

[50] Alison Light, *Common People: In Pursuit of My Ancestors* (Chicago: University of Chicago Press, 2014), 31.

Chapter Four
The Value of Things

Genealogists and writers both work in a world of words. The genealogist pores over records. The writer agonizes over sentences. But both the genealogist and writer have something more tangible than words as their goal. Audible symbols designated by lines and dots, which is all words really are, are only the medium. The genealogist and the writer use that medium in order to create the sense of a solid time and place and people.

I'd spent months researching my third-great-grandparents. They raised eleven children on a small farm in Hamilton County, Ohio, then moved to the outskirts of Cincinnati. I relied on deeds, church records, a marriage license, censuses, city directories, local histories, and newspapers. Then another researcher, a distant cousin, shared a photograph of the couple. Suddenly, I was face to face with them, looking them in the eye. That photo introduced me to my third-great-grandparents in a way that all the months of research had failed to do.

Objects like this have a particular power to convey history because they have an immediacy that words lack. But the value of things isn't just their immediacy. These things can inform our research and our writing. They are themselves a historical record.

Thomas and Nancy Tattershall were a tidy, somber-looking couple, she in a dark, dot-patterned dress with a frilly collar, he in a dark wool suit and a clerical collar. Before seeing the photograph, I had assumed his father was one of the five founding elders of White Oak Christian Church in their rural township of Ohio, but now I realize that it was the younger Thomas.[51] The photo might well have been taken in honor of the event, in 1848. Nancy's hair is parted in the middle and pulled back tightly so that most of it is unseen behind her head. Thomas's hair is straight, parted on the side, and covering his ears in spite of a severe, flipped bob upward that occupies the last few inches. His beard hangs down to the tip of his collar, with no mustache. His hair and beard give him as much of a clergyman's appearance as the collar itself.[52]

That old photo is the most dramatic of a number of images that help bring the couple to life. By 1870, they lived in Cincinnati on the hillside of Boldface Creek and their sons worked at a sawmill.[53] A historic map shows where they lived, beyond the end of Eighth Street near both the sawmill and farmland beyond city limits, where the father of the family continued to work as a farm laborer.[54] Victorian-era photographs illustrate the dynamic growth of the neighborhood into one of Cincinnati's early industrialized slums, but an unexpected painting altered how I thought of the family's new home.

Figure 7. A 19th-century photograph of Thomas and Nancy Isgrigg, possibly taken in 1848 at the time of his ordination as an elder at White Oak Christian Church. Digital image of original shared via personal e-mail.

Henry Lovie painted *View of Bold Face Creek in the Ohio River Valley* in 1858, a few years before the Tattershalls moved there. At the center of the canvas, the creek empties into the Ohio River. The river's opposite bank is in the background, a fenced-in field is in the foreground, and a hillside rises up the right-hand side. It is an entirely pastoral scene with only a couple small buildings at the bottom of the hill along the creek.[55] After looking at the map and learning about this western limit of Cincinnati, I realized that Lovie must have situated himself on or very near the road the Tattershalls would soon call home. If the painter had repositioned himself in the opposite direction, he would have found himself painting a cityscape with a sawmill and a cluster of about forty houses in the foreground and Cincinnati immediately beyond them. Like the painter, the family practically straddled city and country when they moved there.

The value of things for the writer of a family story is the ability to describe directly from a source, rather than just report what the historic record has described. When working from records, writers tend to find themselves wanting more. When working from photos, paintings, and other tangibles, you might find yourself struggling to say all there is to say.

There are a number of things beyond the written record that you should be exploring in order to complete your family story. If your project includes video or illustration, these also will provide an essential visual component.

Figure 8. View of Bold Face Creek in the Ohio River Valley, *an oil painting of the land immediately west of Cincinnati, painted in 1858 by Henry Lovie. Courtesy of Wikimedia Commons.*

VISUAL HISTORY

People have been creating images even longer than they've been keeping written records, so it should come as no surprise that there's a visual record of your family history as well as a written one. The family photos and portraits, the ones that let us look into the eyes of our ancestors, are typically the most compelling. Photography can take us as far back as the mid-19th century and was instantly popular when introduced to the public, but surviving photographs become rarer and rarer the further back in time we research. Painted portraits take us back centuries more but tend to document only the well-to-do.

Although you might not have any luck finding images of your family members much further back than a century, there might still be a useful visual record earlier than that. In the same way that you expand the search of your family's story by looking at the general history surrounding their time and place, you want to make sure to look at the corresponding visual record as well. Etchings and engravings as well as historic photos and paintings can reveal cityscapes, landscapes, and scenes of important moments as well as everyday life.

The search for historical images begins within your own family, including those more distant members met through networking for genealogy. Beyond that, it is little different than your search for historical records. Once you know the place you're interested in, start with local libraries, archives, and historical societies. Even when they don't have the actual images, they typically know where to find them. However, the instinct for librarians and historians is to go for the written records. You'll want to specify that you're also interested in finding relevant images.

The first step to incorporating images into your family story is to analyze them. Answer as many questions as you can about an image from both the image itself and the information you have about it. The National Archives suggests answering these questions:

When was it taken (or made)?
Where was it taken?

Who are the people in it?

What objects are in it, from the small (like the clerical collar) to the large (like the Ohio River or the buildings along Boldface Creek)?

What's happening in it? Is it a posed shot or a candid capture of an event or moment?

Who took it, painted it, etc.?[56]

Hold off thinking about how an image can enhance your family story until you understand as much as you can of the image itself. When you're done looking at images then you're ready to go look at the real thing.

PLACES

I first learned about the world of Civil War reenactment while working for a daily newspaper about twelve miles from a preserved Civil War battlefield. Assigned to cover the 130th anniversary of the battle, I was surprised by the power not so much of the battle re-enactment itself but the bivouac, the neat rows of little canvas tents and the hum of uniformed re-enactors mingling and milling around. Since then, I've been there on a quiet morning. To stand alone in the middle of an old battlefield is to sense its ghosts, but to stand there in the middle of that campsite during the anniversary was to sense something of the time when they were alive.

Telling your family story means creating that sense of what it was really like for those who lived it. The more you can immerse yourself in the tangible experiences they experienced, the better you'll be able to re-create them. There are historic sites as well as preserved natural areas across America and throughout the world. Your family story stands to benefit from discovering and visiting relevant sites, places that your ancestors had a connection to and places that can serve as analogous representations of their lives as well.

GEOGRAPHICAL HISTORY

A map can provide almost as intense a look at a place as a photo provides of a person. You have to bring with you all you know about the place a map represents, but with knowledge of who was where and the nature of the environment both natural and built, a map can bring to life the world of your ancestors. In the fall of 1902, eleven-year-old Earl Tattershall was seriously injured jumping off a freight train he had ridden to Oneonta.[57] Where's Oneonta and why did the boy jump a train to get there? A look at a map reveals Oneonta as an isolated spot on the banks of the Ohio River about fifteen miles upstream from the boy's hometown of Newport (and much closer over land by train). He had probably gone fishing.

To trace the path a child must have taken to get to school or to realize a family's home was across the street from the tavern and just a couple blocks from a wharf is to begin to sense what life was like for your ancestors. Historic maps combined with concrete knowledge of a person's life can inspire ample descriptions grounded on facts never stated point-blank in the historic record. And those Sanborn fire insurance maps, detailed depictions of cities across North America from 1867 to 1950, allow you to explore a city almost as if you were really there.[58]

KEEPSAKES AND TREASURES

If looking at a historic photo allows you to practically look into the eyes of your ancestors then holding an object from your family's past allows you to practically touch them. It doesn't necessarily matter if it's an object of great significance or something mundane. The power is in its tangibility. As with these other things, analyzing the object is the first step. What is the object's history? How did your ancestors use it? Why was it kept and passed on?

Jean Goeke carried a little prayer book with a faux-gold plastic cover at her first communion in the 1930s. Her mother had given it to her, and she in turn gave it to her younger daughter for her first communion in the 1970s. This daughter gave it to her oldest daughter for her first communion in the early 2000s. As an heirloom, the prayer book has a certain importance simply because three generations carried it at this same milestone moment in their lives, a testament to continuity across generations that had seen a great deal of change. However, the latest recipient of the prayer book also discovered a note that had been tucked away within the prayer book's pages. It contained a spiritual reflection written by her great-grandmother to her grandmother, which included, in part:

> ... It is the opinion of many doctors of the church that the Blessed Virgin before she died asked and obtained of her divine Son the freedom of all the Souls who up to that time were in the flames of purgatory. She was accompanied in her solemn assumption into heaven by these souls. Thence she was given the titles of Queen of Mercy, Mother of grace ....[59]

There are a number of things to consider and that could become part of the story of these four generations of women. Based on the weightiness of the note's content, LaDonna Goeke probably gave her daughter the note much later than her first communion. Her daughter valued the note enough to keep it, and placed it in a childhood prayer book she also had valued enough to keep and pass on. Because the note is handwritten, we have more than just LaDonna's words. She wrote with a neat, legible hand, and a textbook rightward lean. Even the loops and curves, that might be taken for personal flourishes, reveal an enduring dedication to the New Palmer cursive she probably learned in school as a girl.

LaDonna died while her daughter was still hospitalized after the birth of that daughter's third child, so the later generations who carried the prayer book with them at their first communions never knew her. However, Jean Goeke related the memory of her mother sitting by the back window of their home when she prayed her daily rosary. The note provides an interesting glimpse into the interior thoughts that might have accompanied this remembered activity.

Good storytelling requires good details. While researching records and artifacts in search of birth, marriage, and death, you should also be taking note of the details that help create an image of the men and women on your family tree. The quotes that give some sense of how they talked. The descriptions that reveal how they looked. The conflicts that begin to reveal what motivated them. The tragedies and triumphs that reveal the burdens they bore and the pride they carried with them. As much as possible, you want to see them as they were and how they lived, or at least to see their surroundings and something of those neighbors who shared a time and place with them. If anything, your family story requires an even greater willingness than your family tree to follow every possible lead. You never know where you're going to find that perfect little detail or that grand inspiration.

---

[51] Ruth J. Wells, *Colerain Township "Revisited,"* unpublished manuscript, undated, Colerain Historical Society, 46.

[52] Photo scan received through private e-mail, 2020.

[53] 1870 U.S. census, Hamilton County, Ohio, population schedule, Cincinnati 21st Ward, p. 98 (printed), dwelling 497, family 782, Thomas Tattershall; digital image of NARA microfilm publication M593, roll1217, *FamilySearch* (https://www.familysearch.org/ark:/61903/3:1:S3HT-DZKQ-15C : accessed 6 April 2023).

[54] R.C. Phillips, *Atlas of the State of Ohio* (New York: H.H. Lloyd & Co., 1868), 55.

[55] Henry Lovie, *View of Bold Face Creek in the Ohio River Valley*, 1858, oil on canvas, Cincinnati Museum Center.

[56] "Analyze a Photograph," National Archives, https://www.archives.gov/files/education/lessons/document-analysis/english/analyze-a-photograph-intermediate.pdf.

[57] "Nearly Killed By Cars," *Cincinnati Enquirer*, 13 October 1902, 9.

[58] Walter W. Ristow, *Fire Insurance Maps in the Library of Congress* (Washington: Library of Congress, 1981), 1-9.

[59] Personal collection of Kathryn Harvey, 2021, Lexington, Kentucky.

Chapter Five
Format

Your research results will help you determine how to tell your family story, both in terms of format and length. There are any number of mediums out there, but start by thinking in terms of three broad formats. Should your family story be told as text, audio, or video? All three will involve writing, so consider text as a default. If there are enough components of your family story that lend themselves to audio–a recorded voice or an important song, for example–then you might want to consider audio. If there are enough components that lend themselves to video–home movies, photographs, or landmarks still in existence–then you might want to consider video.

Within each of these three broad formats, there are things to consider and specific options to choose from.

TEXT

You're already generating documents for your lineage research—reports, charts, family group sheets—so text is probably the most familiar instrument for telling your family story. Print on demand and e-books make even a book-length narrative a realistic possibility. Or you might simply have a number of short family stories that can become attachments to their related family group sheets. Or anything in between. Let content dictate word count. Research your story, plan your story, write your story, and when you know you're done, you'll know how long it should be.

However, you'll want to think about format and appearance before you print. E-book sites like Draft2Digital might provide templates for formatting your e-book. Follow their guidelines to make sure your e-book has a professional look. Formatting for a print version of your book will be entirely different, but print-on-demand companies like Lulu Direct or Kindle Direct Publishing will offer templates for that as well. There also is the option of blogging your family story. This especially suits telling a story in episodes or sharing a variety of short stories over time. Blogging also provides a large potential audience, including people you've never met who are researching the same family lines.

You might decide that an unpublished manuscript version is all you need, especially for something shorter than book-length and for something you're only planning to share with a small audience. You'll still want to think about formatting and binding that gives your finished work durability and a professional appearance. You might opt for the sort of one-inch-margin, double-spaced format that is standard for manuscripts or you might opt for something that gives your manuscript more of a published appearance. Look around and decide what you like, but make an intentional decision about format and hold yourself to it.

One of the hard lessons of life is that regardless of whether or not you can judge a book by its cover, people *will* judge a book by its cover. Unless you are a graphic artist, or know one who is willing to help, you should at the very least work with a free site like Canva to create an attractive book cover. Paying a professional might also be an option to consider, especially if you plan to sell your work.

GENEALOGY JUDE AND *THE DOOR TO YOUR PAST*

Judith Batchelor is a historian and professional genealogist who was already writing for genealogy magazines and family history journals when she decided to start blogging about her family history research. Under the handle *Genealogy Jude*, her blog, *The Door to Your Past* (genealogyjude.com), covers a combination of interesting

Figure 9. Judith Batchelor.

family stories and information about helpful sources she's come across.[60]

She finds that blogging improves her research.

"When writing about your research, you see the gaps," she says.

But she also wants engagement with other researchers. That means promotion can be just as time consuming as writing blog entries. She uses social media to promote her blog entries and has found the most success with her nearly five thousand followers on Twitter (now X).

"Blogging provides a way of telling stories about your family history to preserve them for the benefit of future generations," she says.

With her writing background, Batchelor feels comfortable writing longer articles for her entries—her entry on Victorian-era royal coachman Joseph Osborn ran more than two thousand words and was timed to run soon after the coronation of King Charles III in spring 2023.

Batchelor uses WordPress, the most popular blogging platform on the Internet. Getting started meant jumping in and taking time to learn the platform's ins and outs simply by exploration and trial and error. For example, she quickly learned that footnotes weren't an option for her chosen template, so she decided to use images of her sources with the citation information included as the captions.

She gives this advice to would-be family history bloggers:

• Find what works for you, in terms of timing, length, and emphasis on promotion.

• Write well. Titles, especially, must be written in a way that grabs attention. If you want engagement you must write in an engaging way.

• Tag well. Tagging—the assignment of keywords to your entries—will play an important role in driving potential readers to your blog entries.

• Use pictures in order to break up text, grab attention, and provide the additional information that images are particularly suited to provide.

• Once you've been blogging a while, revisit old entries and promote them again, especially if there's a new relevance, such as the story of Bertie Batchelor's World War I military medal for bravery (originally posted in February) on Great Britain's Remembrance Day in November.

• Focus on what really interests you, because blogging is a commitment that requires sustained attention.

KEITH GREGSON AND *A VIKING IN THE FAMILY*

Keith Gregson is a historian and retired history teacher whose resume includes a substantial bibliography of publications. So it's no surprise that his interest in family history resulted in a number of books and articles as well, including *A Viking in the Family: And Other Family Tree Tales*.

Figure 10. Keith Gregson.

Published by The History Press (United Kingdom), the book includes forty-seven short stories about interesting ancestors discovered by himself, extended family, and various friends and associates.[61]

Gregson had built up a number of his own stories to tell for *A Viking in the Family*, but he knew he needed more. He put out a call for stories from the people he knew and soon had what he needed for a book-length publication. Generally speaking, the stories came to him in good shape so the need for editing was minimal. One of his passions as a history teacher had been to stress the importance of backing up stories with facts, so each family tree story is followed by "The Tale Behind the Tale," a brief explanation of the research and sources that went into the story.

Gregson followed up *A Viking in the Family* three years later with *A Tommy in the Family: First World War Family History and Research*, also published by The History Press and similarly focused on interesting family stories and the research that went into discovering them. He has made his more recent research and publications available free of charge as pdf-format documents through his personal website (keithgregson.com). These include *From Shetland to Keel Square*, about the connection between families in the Shetland Isles and the seaman there who moved to the ports of northeast England to find work; and *Can You Do Nothing to Mend My Broken Heart?*, about the tragic effects of World War I on Sunderland's Ashbrooke Sports Club. "I just sort of bound them as they were, and people were interested in them," he says.

He gives this advice to would-be authors, regardless of whether they're pursuing a publisher or preparing something for self-publication:

• Collect, collate, and deploy. These are the steps that any good historian pursues for publication, Gregson says. Each one requires attention.

• First, assemble all the information you have. "Do what a good historian does," he says.

• Second, organize what you know. "I think you've got to have a kind of mind which can compartmentalize and build up a story."

• Third, write your story. "Write it up as if you're just talking to them as people," he says. "And don't start at the beginning then move to the end. You do the middle then the end then the beginning."

• Re-read. Don't worry about getting everything right on the first draft. Come back to it with fresh eyes.

• Throughout the process, exercise self-discipline and structure. It isn't enough to know the process, you have to hold yourself to it in order to gain the benefit it can potentially offer to the work you're producing.

AUDIO

A spoken word format has the advantage of drawing in sound as a part of your storytelling. It lends itself to a more casual, conversational tone and opens up your potential audience to those who prefer listening to content over reading it. The spoken word also tends to hold audience attention longer than reading does.

You might take a more formal approach, like an NPR-style piece (npr.org), or something with a more spontaneous feel, like the Crime Junkie podcast (crimejunkiepodcast.com). Both require planning and skill. A carefully-scripted narrative has to be performed, not just read in a monotone. A conversational talk has to be organized to avoid rambling. In both cases, the narrator needs to communicate enthusiasm for the topic.

With audio, you're essentially creating a radio show, with its own introduction and format. If you're telling your family story in episodes, you'll want to give episodes a certain consistency, not only in terms of introduction and format but also in terms of a set length of time.

When it's time to record narration, you'll need quality equipment and a quiet place. When you're done recording, you'll need editing software and directions for using it.

To take full advantage of an audio approach, you'll want to incorporate sounds other than your own voice, as appropriate. This can include sound effects, music, and interviews with other people involved in your family history project. Make sure you have proper permissions for anything you use that isn't your own work.

Once you've finished your recording, you'll have a file you can share privately with friends and family or something you can share as a podcast. Podcast hosting sites generally charge a fee, but some, like Podbean, have free options as well.

JACKIE, CHARLOTTE, AND *THIS IS WHAT WE FOUND*

Genealogy had been a family tradition for sisters Jackie Taylor and Charlotte Campanella, so they picked up the habit at an early age. After decades of researching as a team, however, they decided a few years ago to start talking about it with others in the form of a podcast called *This Is What We Found*.[62]

Figure 11. Jackie Taylor, left, and Charlotte Campanella.

Each week, Taylor and Campanella pick a topic, a key ancestor they want to explore. Then they conduct their research separately to prepare for recording, typically touching base about what they've found throughout the week.

"It's a little harder than writing," Campanella says. "You have to say it on the spot after the research, and you have to retain the research to even speak about it."

"But, also, it's definitely more direct and it's more personable," Taylor adds.

Their approach is conversational, spontaneous, and light-hearted.

"We're a little goofy, so I think we try to use that, too," Campanella says.

Their goal isn't just to share what they found. They hope to connect with other researchers pursuing the same lines. Sometimes their listeners have questions, and sometimes they have answers. The last podcast of each month is typically dedicated to a listener suggestion.

That means promoting the podcast is essential. Taylor and Campanella have had the most success finding their audience through history and genealogy message boards dedicated to specific families and places, on *Ancestry* and elsewhere online. With each episode, they focus on the specific family and its place in order to decide how to reach out about that specific episode.

They use Libsyn (thisiswhatwefound.libsyn.com) as their podcasting platform, which allows them to distribute to the outlets they select, such as Spotify and Apple. Campanella just happens to have a recording studio in her house, thanks to her musician husband. But a good microphone plugged into a computer and a little bit of editing to get rid of coughs and other interruptions would typically be enough to make it work.

"It's as spontaneous as it sounds on purpose," Campanella says. "I think people like that."

Taylor and Campanella offer this advice:

• Remain calm and don't worry about whether or not you can talk enough about your topic. "If it's a topic that is really important to you, you'll be able to talk about it," Taylor says. "Charlotte and I have continued to do the show because we love this topic and she and I can talk to each other for hours about it."

• Be ready to put effort into three distinct steps: research, podcasting, promotion. "You have to be the genealogist, the podcaster, and the marketer for your show," Taylor says.

• Get started. "We jumped in head first without really even realizing what would be the benefits of using a platform like podcasting," she says.

VIDEO

Telling your family story as a documentary will require far more than pressing *play* on your phone's camera. While it's true the tools for creating good video are more accessible than ever, putting together quality video will require knowledge of lighting, cinematography, and post production. You'll need shots that illustrate your narration and interviews. Where an expository approach–simply narrating your story–might work well in text or audio formats, lacking accompanying visuals might lead you to give greater consideration to a participatory approach, one that puts you into the picture, as well as others still living.

However, length need not worry you. As with text and audio, your story will dictate length, ranging from a full-length documentary you might post on YouTube, to a series of very short episodes posted over time on TikTok. As filmmaker Betsy Chasse says: "Let your story decide."[63]

NYTN AND *FINDING LOLA*

Danielle Romero was sixteen when she first saw a picture of her great-grandmother Louise Donnelly. Her family had always described Louise as French, from Louisiana. But she didn't "look French." So Romero asked questions. But everyone in the family seemed to have different answers. That prompted her to start researching her great-grandmother's story.[64]

Figure 12. Danielle Romero.

Years later, she was still asking questions, but since she had moved from her hometown near Albany, New York, to Nashville, that meant video conferencing. Soon, Romero found that she had a catalog of video interviews from her questions as well as answers from her research. She was ready to tell the story of her great-grandmother—whose own ancestry was a combination of mixed-race Creole and Native American. Romero decided on a video documentary in order to incorporate her newly-compiled catalog of family interviews.

The result was *Finding Lola* (nytonashville.com), a documentary about a mixed-race woman from Louisiana who married a man from New York in 1925 and moved back there with him when his job was done in Louisiana. She adopted the name "Louise" along the way, passed as white with varying degrees of success, and had eight children, including Romero's grandmother.

Romero's first video interview was of her grandmother, recorded using a cell phone. Over time, her technology improved, as did her technique, but she's glad she didn't wait to get started. Her grandmother died before the project was completed.

"I realized there was something important to me about having this person—her voice—and I wanted to be able to share with my aunts and cousins. And I thought, 'Well, I better figure out how to stitch it together,'" she says.

The result is a forty-five-minute documentary posted on Romero's YouTube channel, NYTN (for New York to Nashville). What began as a video that could be shared with family has now been viewed more than 763,000 times.

As a former history teacher, Romero has always been drawn more to history than genealogy, but the story of her great-grandmother Lola Perot incorporates a great deal of big-picture historical themes, including the narrow definitions of race in the early 20th century and the treatment of minorities both in the Deep South and Upstate New York.

"When I talked to people, they were interested in it, and that was really shocking. And I'm still surprised, honestly, that anyone cares. But I think it's a pretty universal story of just not really knowing where you come from, even if the specifics are different," she says.

Finding Lola incorporates a variety of interviews, but it also includes historic photos, video footage of the places involved, and even text as additional visual elements. An appeal to extended family on Facebook produced an abundance of photographs. Her husband, a musician, wrote music specifically for the documentary.

Romero edited the video, first using iMovie, which came with her Macintosh computer, then later with Final Cut Pro, another Apple product. After interviewing the relatives she knew in New York, she reached out to extended family she had never met in Louisiana, and was surprised to find people who had known her great-grandmother. She traveled to Louisiana to interview them.

"Sometimes we used our iPhone and we met in the local library. It didn't really cost anything, but it was so incredible to do that," she says.

Romero doesn't regret diving in and learning along the way.

"You can become really good with the technical side, but if you don't have the story, I mean, that's what we're all drawn to, right?" she says.

In addition to the documentary, Romero has put together a workbook, *be a good ancestor*, that walks through the process of video interviews. She suggests following these steps:

• Set goals and get organized. Write down the names of all your oldest living relatives. If you aren't comfortable reaching out to them, find another relative who is. Also, be ready to help them with technology they aren't familiar with.

• Prepare for interviews. Start with basic, open-ended questions. You'll be surprised at how much older relatives remember and want to share.

• Record and document. Don't be afraid to learn as you go. The important thing is to get the faces and voices telling their stories.

• Save and share your family story. Romero opted for a YouTube channel, but even an unpublished video file can be kept and shared.

• Reconnect, reflect, and repeat. *Finding Lola* is at times a documentary of family history research in real time. By the time she was recording the last episode of the documentary, she was working with information she didn't even know existed when she was recording the first episode.

"I didn't realize how much value the older members of my family are. They're able to help me understand who I am better. But you have to pursue it," she says.

As the foregoing examples demonstrate, you should let your story, and all the potential material available to tell it, decide whether video, audio, or text best suits it. But always keep your intended audience in mind. For example, if you're hoping to reach an audience beyond your own family, you'll not only need to pick the right format, you'll want to emphasize themes in your narrative that relate to that broader audience. Some family stories are capable of grabbing a broad interest, but they need to be presented in a format to reach a broad audience and crafted with that audience in mind by drawing out the aspects of the story that make it more universal.

    You'll also want to consider your own interests and skills. What challenges are you ready to take on? Bear in mind that the decision to go with audio will still require text and that going with video will still require text and audio. Each move down the list involves adding new challenges, both in terms of elements that will need to be included and skills that you'll need to hone.

---

[60] Judith Batchelor interview with the author, 28 November 2023.

[61] Keith Gregson, interview with the author, 29 November 2023.

[62] Jackie Taylor and Charlotte Campanella, interview with the author, 30 November 2023.

[63] Betsy Chasse, *The Documentary Filmmaking Master Class: Tell Your Story from Concept to Distribution* (New York: Allworth Press, 2019), 16.

[64] Danielle Romero, interview with the author, 27 November 2023.

Chapter Six
True and Good

I can't help but groan a little when I see the phrase, "Based on a true story," at the beginning of a movie. For me, those words have come to mean I'm about to see a grand display of exaggeration, speculation, and outright lying.

Then there's my favorite bookstore's history section. So many titles. So many beautiful covers. And so very boring. One reason so many students hate history is that there isn't enough story in it.

Writing your family history should begin with the conviction that you can tell a true story that engages readers, keeps them pushing forward to the end, and leaves them with a lingering experience of it long after they're done.

I typically go looking for the facts after watching a Hollywood version of a true story, and I rarely find a story that's less interesting than the one I've just watched. Far from it. The complexities, the paradoxes, and the open questions only make the actual history more interesting. I've also spent years sifting through primary documents, and I rarely find the real words of real people from the past as dead dull as the parsing and theorizing they're given so many years later. The immediacy, the particularity, and the color of their language provide insight entirely lacking from most academic analysis.

In short, your family story can be both true and good.

In the last years of the twentieth century, the Board for Certification of Genealogists developed the Genealogical Proof Standard as a way to establish just what constitutes a valid result when researching family lineage. Summarizing the Standard is easy: thorough searches, informative citations, analysis and comparison, resolution of conflicts, and written results.[65] Applying the Standard, however, is tough. But it's worth it. Family trees built using the Genealogical Proof Standard have greater accuracy, verifiable sources, transparent logic, and honest acknowledgement of uncertainties that remain. Applying the Genealogical Proof Standard to all your family research is the key to telling a family story that is true.

Take it as a given that your family story will only state as fact what you have proven as fact. Keep learning the methods of genealogy in order to draw more solid conclusions and to find new information from newfound sources. Use citations, appendices, or a genealogy website to provide sources and proofs for those of your readers who want such things—although, unlike research reports, use endnotes rather than footnotes, to help keep reader attention on the narrative by eliminating distractions at the bottom of the page.

But once you've assembled the facts and you're ready to move from family tree to family history, make sure you tell a good story. You're done fact-finding. Now it's time to spin a tale.

Don't explain how you got there. Just tell what you found. And don't get bogged down in the details of everything you've learned, or how you learned it, to the distraction of what's really interesting.

Here's a little story I have to tell about one of my great-uncles:

> Albert Willmoth lived a varied life, but he reached the height of his career 123 feet above the Ohio River on John A. Roebling's suspension bridge between Covington and Cincinnati. Known as the Human Lizard, Willmoth dived at least twice from the bridge, once in the summer of 1923 and again a year later.[66] He got his professional start as a "fancy and high diver" in 1921, less than a mile upstream on the Louisville & Nashville Railroad bridge between Newport and Cincinnati, diving headfirst into the Ohio to close out the local Salvation Army's fundraising campaign.[67] He mounted the bridge's downstream rail, balanced on the balls of his feet then took off.

"Gliding smoothly, seemingly like a great bird, Willmoth made a half turn and cleanly cut the muddy waters of the Ohio a second after his take-off," the local newspaper observed.[68]

He later made the dive on his own for donations and wagers.

As is so often the case when it comes to choosing a profession, Willmoth's interest started as a boy, when a man drifted into town and startled the locals by jumping off bridges. Willmoth in turn startled his friends by announcing that he was going to jump as well. Against their protests, he made the leap. Years later, when the Salvation Army said it needed a thrill to help attract subscribers, he volunteered to make the dive.[69]

Before making a name for himself as a diver, he had worked as a fourth-generation carpenter, including work with the Army Engineer Corps during World War I.[70] Afterward, he opened a series of taverns, including Eight Mile Tavern and Cafe Albert in Cincinnati, before working as a bricklayer.

He aspired to a political career and served as chairman of the local New Deal Democratic Club, running the committee out of his cafe.[71] But his run for Cincinnati city council ended with him in twentieth place.[72] Later in life, a run for state representative in rural Robertson County, Kentucky, also failed.[73]

His varied life included a variety of wives. Seven of them. Three of them divorced him, one died before him, and two had their marriages annulled, one on the grounds Albert was not yet divorced when they married and the other on the grounds that she had not yet divorced when they had married.[74] He was a drinker who mistreated his wives. His third wife accused him of threatening to kill her prior to her filing for the annulment; a judge issued a restraining order against him, along with the annulment.[75] Willmoth's fourth wife accused him of making appointments and standing her up. When she would go home, she'd find him drunk, and when she protested, he beat her.[76]

Willmoth and his last wife moved thirty-five miles south of Cincinnati to Falmouth, Kentucky, in 1957, where they began living and working at Corral Service Station and Motel. He died of a heart attack while at work there eight months later.[77]

From his seven marriages, he had only one child, but this son later took the surname of his stepfather as his own.[78] Willmoth made a name for himself over the Ohio River, but it was a name his son didn't want. And having spent his life pursuing such a varied career, Willmoth ended it at the age of fifty-nine as a gas station attendant.

There's a lot at work behind this brief story. The first glimpse of Willmoth's bridge-diving career came only from a city directory, in which he listed his occupation as "high diver."[79] The local newspaper took an interest at the time, of course, but reported his name as *Willmott* and *Wilmont*. So, with no details as to what his diving entailed, database searches yielded no result. There it would have remained, a quirky listing

Figure 13. Bridge diving in Cincinnati made news throughout the late 1800s/early 1900s. On 9 June 1890, the Cincinnati Enquirer *depicted a diver from one of the bridges Albert Willmoth later dived from.*

on the family tree with no explanation. Oral history within my own immediate family sent me back to those newspapers with what I needed to find out more.

The story of his wives was equally elusive. I still have found only four official marriage records for Willmoth's seven marriages. Newspapers, death certificates, and court records provided information for the rest.

However, none of that matters. Albert Willmoth was a character. Charismatic, thrill-seeking, grandiose. He was a notable drinker in an age of notable alcoholism, and his ability to catch the attention of women was only the charming side of a man who almost immediately mistreated them once they had married.

From a storytelling perspective, however, diving headfirst into the Ohio River is the beginning of things, even though from a research perspective, it was the end.

Don't tell this story instead:

> I knew Albert Wilmoth must have been a character just from the variety of occupations he listed in various censuses and city directories. He was a carpenter in 1920, a bricklayer in 1930, a restaurant owner in 1940. And then, oddest of all,

was a high diver in the 1923 city directory for Newport, Kentucky. He was my father's uncle and he died before I was born. I just assumed he was being facetious when he listed his occupation as "high diver," and I moved on with my research. After all, his father's occupation was listed as "capitalist" in the 1900 census, at a time when he was working as a carpenter.[80]

Then my middle brother and I got to talking about family at the visitation for our mother's funeral. He told me about a trip he took when he was just a boy with our father to see our grandmother, who hadn't really been a part of our lives. My father was quiet until they were crossing the Ohio River. It was as if once safely out of Kentucky, he could say things that he couldn't say back home. He started talking about the family he grew up with, and largely left behind after he married, including an uncle who had dived into the very river they were crossing to raise money for the Red Cross, although I later learned it was for the Salvation Army.

This is the story genealogists enjoy sharing with other genealogists, and it has real value for us. Stories about the labyrinth of real-life research illuminate the craft of genealogy. After all, it doesn't happen as methodically as conference sessions and our own research calendars suggest. But that isn't the story of Albert Willmoth. The story of Albert Willmoth is the story of the Human Lizard diving from bridges into the Ohio River and the string of women who were, for the most part, as anxious to be rid of him as they had been to marry him.

The greatest writer I ever knew personally was Jane Gentry. She became the Poet Laureate of Kentucky in 2007, but I knew her decades earlier as a professor and staff advisor of a campus literary journal. I was a journalism student learning the trade of a just-the-facts writing profession who joined the literary journal's staff to get some experience as an editor. Part of her job was to teach us what we should be looking for in a quality literary submission.

"Good poetry doesn't tell you what to feel. It makes you feel it," she told us.

Jane Gentry was a great teacher, a beautiful writer, the classiest of Southern ladies, and a good friend. She taught us a lot of valuable lessons that year, but that's the one I remember most. Quite frankly, that alone is enough to have made her a profound influence on me as a writer.

We know what to include in our family story because of the feelings that our research brings out in us. We need to stay in touch with those feelings, to respond to what makes us laugh, what makes us ache, and what makes us say to ourselves, "I need to know more about this." Those feelings help us determine what stories to tell, but when it comes time to tell those stories, we need to make sure we just tell the stories. There's no need to tell readers what to feel about a story or to share the journey we took to compile it. If you tell it well—and that means, for the most part, just the facts—readers will feel what you want them to feel, and they'll feel it more deeply than if you've told them what to feel. That's because good, straight-forward writing creates an image in the minds of readers, and readers respond to that image more deeply than they'll ever respond to instructions about how they're supposed to respond.

That doesn't mean that once you have the facts you're done. Far from it. Good storytelling requires sorting through those facts to find what belongs then choosing the right words to describe them. A good story flows. It sounds spontaneous. But ideally each fact, each word, is intentional. It has been scrutinized and included because it supports the story. It moves the story forward, it sets the story's mood, it makes the reader feel. Don't worry. You've been telling stories your whole life. You've developed good instincts. You already know how to sort through the facts and choose the right words.

When Michael Isgrigg first laid eyes on the Ohio River, it was 1789. He and his family were floating down the river on a flatboat with four officers from Kentucky experienced at traveling through what was then hostile territory. Between them, they were armed with six rifles, ten pistols, two swords, and a musket. When the men heard gobbling one morning, they took a canoe ashore to hunt turkeys. Once on land, the sound of gunfire in the distance was enough to convince them of an imminent Shawnee attack and send them paddling back to the flatboat in such a state that they left behind Isgrigg's fourteen-year-old son. When the father heard his son calling out to them, he began paddling the canoe back to shore, but he had to threaten to knock the captain overboard with his paddle to convince the others to help him.[81]

Everything had changed by the time Michael Isgrigg's granddaughter Nancy and her family had moved to Sedamsville, on the northern bank of that same Ohio River. The Civil War had ended, and the river was now the lifeblood of a powerful economy in the American interior. Hostilities remained, but now in the form of a lawlessness–drinking, gambling, fighting–that pervaded the culture along the Ohio and Mississippi. One of Nancy's sons, Benjamin Tattershall, was convicted of grand larceny in 1874 in Covington, a river town on the Kentucky side of the Ohio.[82] Tattershall's accomplice later became a steamboat captain, but Ben moved 400 miles upstream to Pittsburgh, another thriving river town, after serving his sentence. He was soon arrested on a larceny charge once again, this time tried and sentenced as John Clark, until a tattoo on his right arm, *BF Tattershall* in red and blue ink, revealed his identity.[83]

Today, you can get a feel for what the Ohio River must have looked like both in 1789 and 1874 by visiting some of the more remote places along its banks. It is an expanse of dark water, powerful yet serene, casting a silence on the landscape and offering a vista on its opposite bank like an untouchable mirror image. The river played a pivotal role in the lives of both Michael Isgrigg and Benjamin Tattershall, so a description would be appropriate to include as part of their stories. However, the word choice should be entirely different depending on which man's life story is being told.

For Isgrigg, the Ohio was a dark trail pulling his family into a wilderness that announced its menace in echoes over the water. For Tattershall, it was a sweet-tasting current with an onyx shimmer, constantly luring him toward alcohol and theft. One river, but two descriptions to suit two men interacting with it in different times and circumstances.

Choice of details and choice of words to describe those details have everything to do with evoking the atmosphere of your family story and creating an image of that story that readers can themselves feel and respond to. However, in the same way that you've got to organize your notes before filling out your family tree, you've also got to organize your story before writing your family history.

---

[65] Board for Certification of Genealogists, "About BCG," bcgcertification.org/about.

[66] "Diver to give exhibit: Albert Willmouth will make 123-foot plunge from bridge," *Kentucky Post*, Covington, 6 June 1924, 2C.

[67] "'Lizard' will dive from bridge in S. A. drive." *Kentucky Post*, Covington, 30 April 1921, Section One, 1.

[68] "Albert Willmoth Makes Successful Dive From the Suspension Bridge," *Cincinnati Commercial Tribune*, 30 April 1923, 8.

[69] "Newport Lizard To Dive Into Ohio From the Suspension Bridge Next Sunday From the Covington Side," *Cincinnati Commercial Tribune*, 15 April 1923, 17.

[70] 1920 U.S. census, Campbell County, Kentucky, population schedule, Newport, Enumeration District 18, Sheet 5-A, dwelling 107, family 125, Albert Willmott; digital image of NARA microfilm publication T625, roll 563, *FamilySearch* (https://www.familysearch.org/ark:/61903/3:1:33SQ-GR62-65T : accessed 9 April 2023). "Soldier Wedded," *Kentucky Post*, 21 September 1918, 3.

[71] "Club Indorses Slate: Of Three For Council, Governor Davey For Third Term." *Cincinnati Enquirer*, 24 August 1937, 10.

[72] "Both Sides: Make Same Plea: In Campaign For Votes, 'Mark All Nine.'" *Cincinnati Enquirer*, 19 October 1941, 18.

[73] "Hays and Van Hoose In Senate Bid Again," *Kentucky Post*, 3 February 1955, 1.

[74] Albert Willmoth's wives were: Goldie Benzinger (21 September 1918 *Kentucky Post* wedding announcement), Mary Randolph (7 September 1926 Lawrence County, Ohio, marriage license), Edith M. Cook (27 July 1927 Campbell County, Kentucky, marriage license), Velma M. Brose (29 June 1929 Hamilton County, Ohio, marriage license), Anna Mills (14 December 1936 *Cincinnati Enquirer* wedding announcement), Anna Laura Devon (3 October 1942 Hamilton County marriage license), and Nellie Ellison (19 December 1976 Harrison County, Kentucky, death certificate).

[75] "Court Protects Wife: Husband Ordered Not to Molest Her When Charge is Aired," *Kentucky Post*, 11 November 1927, 1. Kenton County, Kentucky, Circuit Court no. 28854, Edith Willmoth vs. Albert Willmoth, 2 November 1927, Kentucky Department for Libraries and Archives.

[76] "Didn't Keep Appointments," *Cincinnati Enquirer*, 3 November 1936, 5.

[77] Pendleton County, Kentucky, death certificate 58-11580, 9 May 1958, Albert Willmoth, Division of Vital Statistics, Frankfort.

[78] Hamilton County, Ohio, death certificate 018169, 27 January 2005, William F. Simon, Department of Health, Columbus. Simon was born more than three years prior to his mother's divorce from Albert Willmoth.

[79] *Williams' Covington, Newport, and Vicinity Directory* (Cincinnati: Williams Directory Co., 1923), 389.

[80] 1900 U.S. census, Jefferson County, Kentucky, population schedule, Louisville, unpaginated, Enumeration District 118, Sheet 18-B, dwelling 318, family 344, John A. Wilmot; digital image of NARA microfilm publication T623, roll 532, *FamilySearch* (https://www.familysearch.org/ark:/61903/3:1:S3HY-DZJ9-SWS : accessed 12 April 2023).

[81] *Autobiography of Daniel Isgrig*, 9.

[82] Kentucky State Penitentiary, Register of Prisoners 1827-1938, Benjamin Tattershall, received 22 January 1875, Kentucky Department for Libraries and Archives.

[83] Western State Penitentiary, Descriptive List 1878-1882, inmate no. 6822, John Clark alias BF Tattershall, p. 1443, Pennsylvania Historical and Museum Commission, Harrisburg.

Chapter Seven
Before You Write

Choosing the right details and the best way to describe those details is the one half of good storytelling that happens at the level of the individual sentence, and even the individual word. The other half is the broader structure of the story, the theme and plot. That broader structure needs to be coherent. It needs to flow logically from one episode to the next. It needs to push forward to a satisfying end.

That means outlining.

Take a deep breath and stay with me if the term *outlining* makes you think of school papers and a string of capital and lowercase letters and Roman and Arabic numerals. There's no need for any of that. Outlining is simply the process of organizing your family story before you write it.

If you're not convinced of the need for outlining, and want to follow your muse instead—or the example of a favorite author who insists he doesn't outline—listen to Jon Franklin, author of *Writing for Story: Craft Secrets of Dramatic Nonfiction by a Two-Time Pulitzer Prize Winner*. Although his focus is narrative nonfiction in general, his observation applies:

"I don't care what you've heard, or what your literature teacher said, *or even what the writers themselves said*. Every writer of any merit at all during the last five hundred years of English history outlined virtually everything he wrote," Franklin writes. "That's why I so smugly assert that Hemingway, Steinbeck and Shakespeare used outlines. I've read their stuff, and it has integrity–that quality of all hanging together, and being an inter-related, organic whole."[84]

Your outline begins with that overall theme discussed in the first chapter. The theme is crucial to understanding the direction the story will take, the details that will be included, and where in the story they'll go. It will determine the steps your story takes and the place where it ends up.

Because most family stories are multi-generational histories, there's a good chance your outline will place things chronologically, but not necessarily.

Approaching a family history as a memoir of your own discovery, for example, will probably begin in the present. From there, it might move steadily backward in time or move here and there based on the chronology of your research. If there's a particular puzzle to solve, you might approach it something like a mystery, which is simply a way of telling a story in non-linear bits in order to place the big reveal at the end. Or you might have decided to write the story of your family during one pivotal moment, the Great Depression, for example. In that case, your family history will tell the story of multiple lives and events that happened simultaneously.

Outlining, in these cases, will require more than just placing story developments on a timeline. You'll need to find another logical way to sequence your story.

Regardless, the outline should establish how to organize and present your story.

Telling the story of my family during World War II, for example, means organizing it to juxtapose two very different people whose families and hometowns embody the era in very different ways.

> Theme: World War II brings a man and woman together from backgrounds so different they never would have met each other without the war.
>
> Intro: Wapakoneta, Ohio, and Newport, Kentucky, embody the age in different ways.
> • Wapakoneta: victory gardens along the Auglaize River just beyond the backyard of Mom's home; a cozy small town in Middle America.

- Newport: street urchins swimming in the Licking River, including Dad; city still run by crime syndicate from Prohibition days.

Goekes
- Father converts local factory for munitions production
- Brother finishes up at military school and goes to Army
- Mom and her sister at school

Tattershalls
- Sister dies of consumption shortly before the war, and grandmother dies of malnutrition in 1941.
- Father leaves family for a former showgirl from one of the clubs/casinos
- Dad drops out of high school to support family, joins Army at 17

After the war
- College for Mom (family expectation/custom)
- College for Dad ... G.I. bill (first generation)

Marriage and family
- New kind of life for Dad ... prosperity/white collar/business travel
- New kind of life for Mom ... leaving hometown and family

There are plenty of details that would make their way into the story of my parents in and around the World War II period. Among other things, those details would need to demonstrate how and why my father, from a poor, broken household, ended up remembering his childhood at least as fondly as my mother remembered hers. This initial outline begins to tell me where those details belong.

The biggest challenge is where to begin and where to end. You might want to decide on both of these first. In fact, once you've decided on the ending, you might want to outline your family story backward from there (and you might want to write it that way, too). Both the beginning and end need to attach to your theme, with the beginning introducing, or at least suggesting, everything that will follow and the ending resolving what was introduced in the beginning.

From there, think in terms of big chunks–the beginning, the end, and maybe two big chunks that connect the two. If you're outlining backward from the ending then decide what story development should immediately lead to your ending. What development leads to that development? If working from the beginning, make sure that each development moves logically from what went before it and pushes the story logically toward its end.

You've started with big chunks, the large movements of the story. Now outline within those big chunks with the large movements within each particular chunk, and so on until you have a complete flow, chapter by chapter and scene by scene from beginning to end.

The more detailed your outline, the more certain you'll be that you're heading in the right direction when you start to write; this allows you to focus on word choice and imagery. Every major moment in your story will already have its place, supporting the theme of the story and driving the plot forward.

As you researched your family history, you undoubtedly will have compiled a list of anecdotes and details that you just know you want to include in your story. Set it aside. Once you've finished your outline, put the list in front of you. Take a look at the outline to see what from the list has already made its way into your story. Take a look at the list and see what's left that might still have a place on the outline. Then take one last look at the list to see what doesn't belong and set it aside for some other narrative.

This is the rigorous process of storytelling. It begins with research into the characters and events plucked from your family tree. It continues with your consideration of the themes that tie together what you've found. It then enters the sweaty task of outlining, and ends with the actual writing, sentence by sentence and word by word.

---

[84] Jon Franklin, *Writing for Story: Craft Secrets of Dramatic Nonfiction by a Two-Time Pulitzer Prize Winner* (New York: Atheneum, 1986), 82-83.

Conclusion

We research our family histories to satisfy our own curiosity about our past, but we quickly find that we want to share what we've found. We share our stories over the dinner table with our families and at workshops and meetings with fellow enthusiasts. These stories have as much value as the lineages we document and organize so scrupulously. Therefore, we should pass on the stories as thoughtfully as we pass on the lineages. They are the anecdotes and struggles and accomplishments of our ancestors as seen through the eyes of those of us who have worked so hard to discover them.

Telling your family story requires its own kind of research: a look at historic records, places, and objects with an eye toward storytelling. Filling out your family tree deserves an effort that incorporates the best practices of the professional genealogist. Likewise, telling your family story deserves an effort that incorporates the best practices of the dedicated storyteller. The result might be only a few pages shared here and there with siblings and cousins. It might be a blog or a podcast or a documentary available online for anybody who takes an interest. It might be a full-length book, self-published, privately shared, or maybe even accepted by a publishing house.

Regardless, your family history is a story worth telling and, therefore, a story worth telling well.

FAMILY STORY WORKSHEET

I want to tell a story about: _____

CHARACTERS: 1. 2. 3. 4. 5.	PLOT: 1. conflict: 2. development: 3. resolution:

Theme: _____

Setting: _____

Sources:
1. _____ 2. _____

3. _____ 4. _____

5. _____ 6. _____

TEXT FORMAT: Platform: Images/illustrations:	AUDIO FORMAT: Platform: Tech needs: Voices/interviews: Additional sound (effects, music etc.):	VIDEO FORMAT: Platform: Tech needs: Voices/interviews: Additional sound: Additional video:

OUTLINE:
1. Opening: _____

2. Development I: _____

3. Development II: _____

4. Development III: _____

5. Closing: _____

Index

A
affective history, 29-31, 47
American Revolution, 1, 20
Arnow, Harriette Simpson (*Seedtime on the Cumberland*), 20
artifacts, 48-49
audio recording, 56-58

B
Batchelor, Judith (*Genealogy Jude*), 52-54
biography, 5, 6, 19, 35
blogging, 10, 51-54
book publishing, 13-14, 51, 54-55
Bragg, Rick (*Ava's Man*), 11
Brontë, Charlotte (*Jane Eyre*), 10-11

C
California Gold Rush, 7-9
Campanella, Charlotte (*This Is What We Found*), 57-58
Centennial histories, 27-29
characters, 6-7, 9, 11, 49-50
Chasse, Betsy (*The Documentary Filmmaking Master Class*), 59
city directories, 66-68
Civil War, 15, 22, 29, 47
conflict, 7-8, 26

D
diaries, letters, and memoirs, 3, 9, 22-23 (Calvin Morgan Smith), 39-40 (John Roberts on the *Clio*)
difficult themes (alcohol and abuse), 15

E
ending, 11, 76

experimental archaeology, 30-31

F
foreshadowing, 10-11
Franklin, Jon (*Writing for Story*), 73

G
Genealogical Proof Standard, 19, 63-64
genealogical/historical societies, 21-22, 23 (Hawkins County, Tenn.), 46
Gentry, Jane, 68-69
Gregson, Keith (*A Viking in the Family*), 54-55
Grigsby, William H. (*Genealogy of the Grigsby Family in Part*), 12-13

H
Hamilton, Nigel (*How To Do Biography*), 5, 39
Hardy, Jeremy (*My Family and Other Strangers*), 14
Heyerdahl, Thor (*Kon-Tiki*), 31
history, 5, 6, 19, 35
Holmes, Richard (*Footsteps: Adventures of a Romantic Biographer*), 30

K
Kendall, Reese (*Pioneer Annals of Greene Township*), 27-29
Klam, Julie (*The Almost Legendary Morris Sisters*), 15

L
lawsuits, 19-20 and 26 (depositions), 25-26, 37-38, 67

libraries, 21-22, 24 (Rockcastle County Public Library), 25, 29, 46, 61
Library of Congress, 24, 27
Light, Alison (*Common People: In Pursuit of My Ancestors*), 14, 40
Lovie, Henry (*View of Bold Face Creek*), 44-45

M
maps, 47-48
marriage records, 28, 67
Maya, Sarah (*Thinking About History*), 5
Mexican-American War, 22
microhistory, 14-15
military records, 20

N
newspapers, 23-25, 33-35, 36 (*Genius of Liberty*), 65-67

O
opening line, 11, 76
oral history, 20-22, 33, 61, 67
outlining, 73-77

P
paintings, 44-47
photographs, 43-47
plot, 10, 11, 73, 76
podcasting, 10, 56-58

R
Romero, Danielle (*Finding Lola*), 59-62

S
setting, 9, 30, 47, 70-71

T
Taylor, Jackie (*This Is What We Found*), 57-58
theme, 12-15, 73-74, 76
timelines, 11, 35, 39

V
video production, 10, 58-62

W
War of 1812 (British aliens), 36-38
writing style, 10, 68-71

www.ingramcontent.com/pod-product-compliance
Ingram Content Group UK Ltd.
Pitfield, Milton Keynes, MK11 3LW, UK
UKHW020916170325
5022UKWH00040B/736